MARKETING RETURN ON INVESTMENT

ZHOUSTIFY
Written by Kamaldeep Singh; CEO & Founder
Edited by Jasmine R. , Zayn M. & Maria L.

TABLE OF CONTENT

INTRODUTION..1

CHAPTER 1
Understanding ROI Principles..................................6

CHAPTER 2
GETTING THE ROI BASICS......................................13

CHAPTER 3
MARKETING ROI DIFFERENT.................................18

CHAPTER 4
MORE MEASURABLE THAN EVER.........................20

CHAPTER 5
MARKETING ROI PROCESS 23

CHAPTER 6
MEASURING RETURN ON INVESTMENT............24

CHAPTER 7
ADOPTING THE MARKETING ROI PROCESS.......32

CHAPTER 8
MANAGING CORPORATE-LEVEL PROfiTABILITY 38

CHAPTER 9
THE MEASUREMENT PROCESS...54

CHAPTER 10
THE IMPLEMENTATION PROCESS 61

CHAPTER 11
MARKETING EFFECTIVENESS: MORE THAN JUST ROI 68

CHAPTER 12
LINK CUSTOMER ASSET TO FINANCIAL PERFORMANCE.80

CHAPTER13
MARKETING ASSET MROI SCENARIO................................94

CHAPTER 14
MARKETING BY THE NUMBERS: Optimization................100

CONCLUSION...107

INTRODUCTION

The sole purpose of marketing is to get more people to buy more of your product, more often, for more money. That's the only reason to spend a single nickel, pfennig, or peso. If your marketing is not delivering consumer's to the cash register with their wallets in their hands to buy your product, do not do it.

SERGIO ZYMAN

The proper use of marketing ROI measurements can compare investment options as diverse as a direct marketing campaign, a dedicated sales force, a retail distribution channel, and an Internet marketing campaign. Marketing ROI analysis can scale from a tag line's incremental value on an envelope to implementing a multimillion-dollar enterprise CRM marketing initiative. It can be used to compare the ROI of a price reduction to a marketing initiative that includes a free offer.

The concepts and examples cover marketing communications and the need for more proactive management to connect investments with incremental returns. For our purposes, marketing is defined as all activities, including sales and advertising, to influence customer behaviors toward generating a financial transaction.

The presentation of the marketing ROI concepts is intended to apply across a broad range of industries and applications. There are differences in how marketing is measured and differences in terminology (which you may need to watch for when reading the book). The underlying principles should be valid regardless of industry. It should also be noted that there are limitations to the effectiveness of marketing ROI practices.

One of the foundations for guiding better market-ing investments is that measurements and analysis will effectively predict future investments' returns. Company's that have low-quantity, high-value customers, are subject to less predictability. The same applies to market initiatives that generate low sales volume.

Measuring the value of a single speaking engagement at a conference or assigning a large team to pitch a single client over a year may not be possible. The intention is to improve the measurement of the financial value of marketing investments wherever possible and recognize that other decisions will still need to be subjective or rely on nonfinancial value.

Another key assumption underlying the marketing ROI principles is that companies will obtain the data necessary to complete the ROI analyses presented. Companies do not have perfect knowledge of the financial activity surrounding marketing initiatives. Still, by understanding the benefits of marketing ROI techniques, it may be easier to justify the actions necessary to improve knowledge in this area. Some ROI concepts will not be effective for certain companies based on their lack of access to the right information.

The goal is to identify what can be implemented in your current environment and how you can make improvements to support further implementation of the marketing ROI process.

There is tremendous opportunity to impact profitability at the campaign, customer, and corporate levels. The information presented here will provide insight to executives, marketers, financial managers, and research analysts. For those readers who want to easily gather the insight necessary to unlock the company's profit potential, I suggest you glance over the formulas and calculations. Those who want to understand the logic behind the concepts or implement specific tools and techniques should be attentive to the calculations.

The concepts presented here should advance the knowledge and understanding of marketing ROI throughout the industry. This is one more step in establishing more effective marketing measurements by building on many quality sources' insights and experience. While writing this book, I have evolved my concepts significantly. Hopefully, others will take these concepts even further and continue to forge the path to better profits.

MROI DEFINED

MROI is the financial value attributable to a specific set of marketing initiatives (net of marketing spending), divided by the marketing 'invested' or risked for that set of initiatives. MROI (aka ROMI) is a relatively new metric. It is not like the traditional 'return-on-investment' metrics because marketing is a different kind of investment. ROI metrics for a firm or SBU performance are almost always annual returns. Other uses of ROI, such as the return on specific financial investment, often leave unspecified the time required to generate the return. Marketing spending is typically expensed in the current period, and, usually, marketing spending will be deemed as justified if the MROI is positive and exceeds the firm's 'hurdle rate.'

More specifically, MROI is the dollar-denominated estimate of the incremental financial value to the entity generated by identifiable marketing expenditures, less the cost of those expenditures as a percentage of the same expenditures:

Unlike other types of investments, marketing funds are rarely tied up in inventories, fixed assets or receivables, and most marketing expenditures come from what otherwise would be liquid funds. Therefore, great care will need to be taken to validate comparisons between the ROI of marketing with other ROI estimates. Some marketing actions are similar to other investments; however, in many cases, they generate revenue and profit returns over multiple years, building cumulative impact and creating assets with future value.

More transparency in reporting these outcome types will help identify the situations under which these comparisons and other applications of MROI are more or less appropriate. The next section addresses these complexities.

THREE COMMON SOURCES OF VARIATIONS IN MROI CALCULATIONS

Although the maths is simple, the meaning and significance of the MROI metric is anything but straightforward. Below we will discuss some important sources of variations that we have identified in how MROI is estimated and reported. Our discussion is intended to support the marketing field's efforts to generate transparent and reliable metrics that can be used to assess and report marketing productivity and motivate an objective-maximizing allocation of resources among competing marketing activities. As such, sources of variations are important and should be fully disclosed when marketers report and apply MROI to decisions.

We have classified these three sources of variations into three categories: (A) methods of valuing marketing returns, (B) scope/ granularity of spending evaluated, and (C) range of spending for which the MROI is calculated.

A. Methods for valuation of marketing returns

The most straightforward of marketing returns used in calculating MROI is the profit margin generated from incremental sales. This is what we have termed a baseline-lift valuation, based on the ability to establish a reasonable measure of the lift over a baseline level of existing sales, attributable to a specific marketing initiative. A slight variation of this is reporting incremental revenue as the return in place of profit. When profit margins are unknown or undisclosed, this calculation is a useful interim step to calculating MROI, although it does not have the precision needed to optimize spend levels. When only incremental revenue is known, we still consider it a baseline-lift valuation but recommend reporting this as 'revenue MROI' to distinguish it from a net profit impact.

It may also be useful when comparing the marketing productivity of two alternative marketing initiatives for the same product or service.

The next two forms of valuation are necessary to account for outcomes when the sales lift is unknown. The first is a funnel conversion outcome, where the valuation of marketing returns involves projecting incremental sales by applying historical or estimated funnel conversion rates. The second is a comparable cost valuation, which considers the financial outcome of cost savings or opportunity cost differences as the marketing investment return.

B. Scope/granularity of marketing spending evaluated (full marketing mix versus individual campaigns/tactics)

MROI measures can assess a single marketing tactic's financial impact or an integrated combination of many tactics, including the full marketing mix. The granular extreme would be ROI measures for a specific search advertisement, an e-mail campaign, or a specific offer within a direct mail campaign.

The other extreme is obtaining ROI measures for the full marketing mix or integrated marketing activities such as the Intel Inside campaign. This multi-year effort would include market research, logo design and revisions, cooperative advertising rebates and all media. As the scope of the marketing efforts included in a particular MROI measure increases, it becomes more important to assess substitute, interaction, and feedback effects among the marketing mix elements. Evaluating a combination of mix elements can lead to a quite different valuation from the sum of separate return calculations.

C. Range: total, incremental or marginal returns

Holding constant the scope and granularity of evaluated activities, there is an important distinction between reporting total, incremental or marginal MROI). Total evaluates return on all spending, incremental for a specified additional spending 'increment,' and marginal is the estimated return on the 'last dollar' of marketing spending.

Total and incremental MROI is typically easier to estimate and often results from A/B testing or models that use linear response functions. Evaluating the marginal returns to spending is more challenging and, except for complex and expensive experiments, will usually involve models that include nonlinear response functions. Conceptually and practically, these three types of returns are different and should not be compared. Although diminishing returns will eventually be encountered, there is no general rule as to which of the three measures of MROI will be higher or lower.

CHAPTER 1

UNDERSTANDING ROI PRINCIPLES

PROFIT IS THE GOAL, ROI IS THE MEASURE

How a company manages its marketing bud-get drives how well the marketing organization can perform and how well the company can perform. Shareholders expect the company to maximize profits so they can achieve the highest possible returns from their investments. The company maximizes profits by maximizing sales revenues, minimizing overhead expenses, maximizing gross margins, and managing its investments to an appropriate level of risk and expected returns.

The ultimate purpose of marketing is to generate profitable sales, and it is to the benefit of shareholders, executives, and marketers to manage the budget as an investment. Consider that return on investment (ROI) is calculated for large capital expenditures and technology implementations.

The profits from productivity and incremental sales are much more difficult to estimate and measure. Marketing, including the communications, advertising, sales, and distribution functions, is directly responsible for driving profits into the company by selling to customers, and there is no longer room for excuses. As Sergio Zyman, former chief marketing officer of Coca-Cola, clearly summarized in his book, The End of Marketing As We Know It, and the "sole purpose of marketing is to get more people to buy more of your product, more often, for more money. Every strategy and the tactical decision should be intended to increase profits. It is completely reasonable, and highly beneficial, to expect a return on investment for each incremental marketing dollar spent.

Companies must maximize profits over the long term, and marketing investments must do the same. Goals are set by the company to provide a common vision and purpose. Measurements are then aligned with the goals to track actual performance relative to the goals and provide feedback to guide future decisions. While profits are necessary to stay in business and satisfy shareholder expectations, executive's must have a vision and purpose beyond just profits to maintain its success. Ultimately, their broad goals for quality, customer satisfaction, new product development, and employee satisfaction should all lead back to sustaining and growing long-term profits.

With profits as the goal and the marketing budget managed as an investment, ROI must emerge as the primary marketing measurement. The advanced concepts around marketing ROI can provide significant financial control to corporate executives while also empowering marketing managers. The marketing ROI process can provide a subjective view of long-debated issues such as prioritizing retention versus acquisition marketing.

The budgeting process can be streamlined and modified to deliver profit optimization truly. You will find no better way to tap into missed profit opportunities than to move farther down the path of marketing ROI measurements.

The Power of Marketing ROI

The most powerful and useful marketing measure is the return on investment, which can relate the total investment made to the total return generated from that investment. ROI can be modified to reflect the relative importance of short- or long-term profits. It is one of the few marketing measurements that can measure and compare diverse marketing efforts with consistency across large organizations. Above all, accurate ROI measures and clear corporate guidelines, can be relied upon to steer the optimal marketing decisions.

Think of ROI measures as intelligence that can be used in strategic and tactical development of marketing initiatives. Marketers rely on all forms of intelligence: customer needs, market conditions, competitive activities, and campaign performance history to improve marketing effectiveness. ROI projections can serve as intelligence into the profit potential. It provides insight into the value that an initiative, strategy, or investment can deliver.

Marketers who can embrace these key principles of marketing ROI have much to gain.

- **ROI is the ultimate measure for guiding marketing investments**. Many other measures provide tremendous insight and intelligence and are critical for making strategic and tactical marketing decisions. Decisions such as improving customer relationships and loyalty, maximizing customer lifetime value, increasing customer satisfaction, or decreasing acquisition costs cannot effectively guide each marketing investment and maximize profits without incorporating the ROI measure.

- **Marketing ROI is unique**. The standard ROI measure could not be simpler. It comes down to how much more money you end up with (your return) than what you invested. Unlike typical large capital investments, marketing investments are made up of many small investment decisions. This means that decisions are not just for selecting marketing programs but also for determining how each incremental dollar should be invested.

- **Marketing ROI must be a primary measure used by companies and organizations to remain competitive.** Applying these techniques to guide marketing investments and marketing strategies will benefit every organization. Each organization has a finite marketing budget and should apply these principles to generate the greatest return on its investment. Those organizations that have a greater purpose than maximizing profits, including nonprofit companies and select for-profit companies, must still pay close attention to ROI to best guide investments that will ensure financial survival.

- **Marketing ROI is most beneficial with executive-level involvement.** The benefits of ROI analysis and planning extend to all levels of a company; however, the major impact on profits can only come with a corporate level commitment. Company executives can improve profits by using ROI in the budget allocation process. They also can set expectations, define standards, and empower their marketing team to drive the right decisions on how marketing investments are made.

The corporate mindset has already begun to shift from treating the marketing budget as an expense to treating it as an investment. Additional effort is needed to manage this investment in such a way to sustain the best and grow the business. Improving return-on-marketing investments can be accomplished by using the ROI measure as a tool for planning, measuring, and optimizing marketing strategies.

SHORTFALLS IN ALTERNATIVE MARKETING MEASUREMENTS

Marketing measurements other than ROI show only a piece of the total picture. These measurements often present great insights that can lead to better marketing strategies; however, these are typically not complete enough for guiding marketing investment decisions toward the greatest profits.

Common marketing measures, such as cost per sale, sales conversion rates, and customer value, are missing either expense or return information, making these poor choices for critical marketing decisions. Cost-per-sale and sales conversion rates do not consider that different marketing efforts may attract customers with different values. Setting customer value as the primary measure independent of an ROI analysis does not consider the marketing expense. The fact that pursuing the highest-value customers is not always the most profitable form of marketing.

The term customer lifetime value (CLV) is used differently in different industries. ROI is dependent on capturing the future stream of profits that result from a specific investment, which will be referred to as incremental customer value (ICV) throughout this book. The most accurate references to CLV capture the entire flow of current and future investments and profits. This measure works much like the ROI calculation for an aggregated set of campaigns. Some industries, such as book clubs, use very consistent marketing and rely on CLV measures that already incorporate ROI calculations.

However, for most companies, this form of CLV does not align with the decision-making process since each campaign's decisions are made independently of one another instead of as a preset series of marketing activities for each customer.

The Accenture research study found that four marketing performance measures were used most commonly—response rate (79%), revenue generation (78%), customer retention (69%), and profit generation (66%). Each measure is important, and all are essential in generating ROI measures. As demonstrated throughout this book, the ROI measure provides marketers with tremendous decision-making and planning capabilities.

ADDRESSING PROFIT PRESSURES

In both good and bad economies, companies make extensive efforts to generate greater profits, which are increased by decreasing expenses, increasing sales, or improving margins. Implementing or improving your use of ROI to guide marketing investments can strengthen your profit potential without increasing your marketing budget.

When the economy was booming, Internet companies spent huge marketing budgets to very quickly build market share. Granted, there was no historical precedent for the true value of quickly building market share. However, more prudent ROI analysis in the planning stage could have made it clear to many failed companies that their expectations for generating future profitable returns were never really given their customer-acquisition costs.

MARKETING ROI: THE NEXT WAVE FOR CRM

Corporate CRM initiatives can significantly benefit from integrating more advanced marketing ROI measurements and tools. CRM technology has been a major expense at many large corporations, and most of these companies are struggling to see the payback. The next wave of activity around CRM will come from efforts to leverage the existing technology to generate profits. There are many synergies between CRM strategies and ROI measurement practices. CRM systems often contain critical information necessary for improving ROI measures, and ROI analysis can guide CRM marketing efforts.

ROI contributes to the advancement of CRM initiatives in the following ways:

- Spending limits can be established at the customer level based on-projected value.
- The value of retaining incremental customers through customer-loyalty programs can be assessed and aligned with the appropriate investment level.
- The ROI measure provides the necessary insight to balance retention and acquisition spending.
- Aggregated ROI analysis can support greater integration between marketing programs using Customer Pathing strategies.

UNDERSTANDING THE KEY CHALLENGES

Measuring ROI does have its challenges, as confirmed by the high percentage of marketing executive is reporting difficulties in the Accenture survey. The major challenges that face companies working toward more accurate and useful ROI marketing measurements are:

• **Generating reliable future value projections**. Customer behavior is not always predictable in today's fast-changing markets, and marketers need to make quick decisions that do not allow time for tracking actual purchase behaviors. Some companies capture only immediate purchase value for their ROI analysis. More and more companies are developing some form of CLV, but that may not always align with the measure necessary for an ROI analysis of specific marketing investment.

• **Getting access to data**. The total value generated from a marketing investment could include immediate purchases, future purchases, future customer service expenses, retention rates, and referrals. Marketing organizations do not always have access to this information, leaving gaps in the analysis.

• **Standardizing measurements, values, and practices**. Corporate standards for ROI calculations, values, and practices allow for greater accuracy and consistency between marketing groups across the organization. Without corporate standards in place, each marketing group is likely to create its version of an ROI formula that best suits its needs and success criteria without maximizing corporate profits.

- **Establishing cost-effective measurement processes.** While experimental tests and research studies may be effective forms of capturing critical values, the reality is that the cost to measure performance must be a worthwhile investment as well. This means that certain marketing efforts will have gaps when the measurement cost is not justified.

- **Establishing valid control groups.** Measuring the impact of marketing campaigns on behaviors and transactions often requires a control group to compare the pattern of behaviors without the marketing campaign. Many marketing efforts, such as those broadcast in mass media, make it impossible to establish valid control groups.

- **Matching results back to the appropriate marketing initiative in multichannel marketing environments.** Marketers rely on multiple contacts to generate sales, and customers rely on multiple channels for information, service, and transactions. Measuring the ROI on a specific marketing investment within multichannel campaigns can be quite complex.

- **Allocating expenses.** Marketing expenses such as creative or development costs need to be captured but must not deter investment in developing new marketing programs and innovations.

- **Understanding residual value.** Those marketing investments that impact future marketing activities do not fit in the standard ROI measurement process. This value must be identified and understood to drive the best investment decisions.

- **Organizational barriers, such as compensation structures.** The existing processes and internal culture include many barriers to the effective use of ROI measurements. Organizational barriers are presented in detail later in this chapter.

- **Total sum approach.** When calculating results, marketers tend to identify and assume profits that show up in other marketing programs or sales channels, without ensuring that those same results are not double-counted. The sum of individual campaign returns and investments should net fairly close to the total profits and budget when marketing ROI measurements are managed properly.

So how do you address these challenges to use ROI more effectively? It is necessary to understand the degree of impact that each challenge could have on your environment. The goal is to gain greater insight for making strategic decisions and prioritizing marketing investments, so the first checkpoint must be on the reliability of the ROI analyses. Once the process can be trusted to provide good information, there can be further improved.

Most of these challenges can be managed by technology, best practices, and behavior shifts. Technology helps companies move past many of the data and analysis challenges and will only get better as users of ROI marketing measures define their needs to the information technology (IT) organization. Best practices for improving ROI measures continue to be introduced, and this book presents approaches for many of the challenges listed. Behavior shifts from marketing campaign managers to senior executives will take time but will happen if supported with tools, training, and incentives.

CHAPTER 2

GETTING THE ROI BASICS

Return on investment (ROI) is a financial measurement. ROI analysis is used to assess and guide many different forms of corporate and personal investments. However, as mentioned in the previous chapter.

ROI is frequently used incorrectly and inaccurately. Before getting into the specific ways ROI is customized for use in marketing, let's first establish a foundation of understanding around the ROI formula by starting with the very basics.

ROI is presented in the form of a percent so that a positive number indicates a financial gain from the investment, and a negative number indicates a financial loss. When the gross margin is equal to the marketing investment, the ROI is 0 percent, and the investment is considered breakeven.

The marketing investment includes all of the expenses put at risk to market the product, service, or company. The return is all of the financial gains beyond the initial investment that is attributed to that investment. It represents the present value of the inflow of revenues and outflow of expenses that result directly from the investment made.

The term gross margin represents the present value of incremental profits and expenses in the calculation of return. More detail will be provided on how gross margin is calculated for marketing measurements.

KEY FINANCIAL CONCEPTS

the following key financial concepts are essential for ensuring that your company's ROI measures align with the right marketing investment decisions. This is not an attempt to turn marketers into financial experts but to present perspectives on how customer behaviors driven by marketing investments translate into profits for the company.

NET PRESENT VALUE

Net present value (NPV) is very important for reflecting the time value of money. Since the ROI measure will ideally capture the full impact of marketing investment, it may need to include profits and expenses that extend over time. Profits generated in future periods are not as important or valuable to a company as profits are delivered immediately. This future cash flow can be discounted monthly, quarterly, or annually, depending on how much relative value a company places on cash in current versus future periods.

The gross margin within the ROI equation is based on the NPV of the stream of profits and expenses that result from the marketing investment. This creates an accurate view and an equitable comparison between marketing campaigns that generate returns over different periods. In the examples presented in this book, NPV calculations dis-count cash flow on an annual basis unless otherwise specified.

Gross Margin

The gross margin represents the financial contribution coming back to the company once the marketing investment has been made. The sales revenue minus the fully loaded cost of goods to produce the product or service, minus any costs related to the sale. Since this flow of income and expenses will occur over time, the gross mar-gin must be converted into NPV

Gross Margin NPV (Revenue Cost of Goods Incremental Expenses)

The cost of goods sold captures fixed costs and variable costs such as materials, manufacturing, labor, and overhead costs allocated based on a percentage of revenues. Incremental expense represents variable costs specific to the sale or set of new customers acquired, such as order processing, fulfillment, and customer service. The actual marketing expense is not deducted from the gross margin, so the gross mar-gin represents all of the profits generated, including the marketing investment's recovery.

Discount Rate

The discount rate is used within the NPV calculation. It is the rate by which the future profits and expenses are discounted to represent a comparable present value. Too often, marketers using ROI set this rate without much consideration. It will vary by company and requires input from the finance department.

The discount rate reflects the rate at which the company can borrow money and the risk associated with its performance expectations. Large, established companies with a good credit history will use a lower discount rate than newly formed ventures that could be considered high risk. Strategically, the discount rate can be used to align the ROI measure with the company's priority for short-term or long-term profits.

Incremental Customer Value and Customer Lifetime Value

Since the term customer lifetime value (CLV) is used so differently within the industry, the term incremental customer value (ICV) will be used in this book to represent the net present value of the income flow generated by a customer (or segment of customers) as a result of the specific marketing investment being measured. To calculate ROI, ICV must include only the stream of profits and expenses that a customer or segment of customer's will generate for the company without additional investment beyond the investment being measured. The ICV must be matched with the incremental investment.

CLV will be used to represent the total of all investments made and the total of all returns generated throughout that customer's lifetime. Individual marketing campaigns may show that some investments do not generate enough ICV to be considered profitable. The entire flow of campaigns to a customer is profitable, as measured by the CLV.

They use the term potential value to represent the total NPV of gross margin the customer can spend with the company by earning a 100 percent share of the customer and growing its total spending. The actual value is most relevant to ROI measurements of past performance. The potential value of a customer, which is very significant to the development of profitable marketing strategies, can influence the ROI projections based on the potential profits earned by different customer groups.

ROI Threshold or Hurdle Rate

The ROI threshold, also known as the "hurdle rate," is the minimum ROI level for which a company will make investments. For example, if a company's ROI threshold is 25 percent, funding will be provided for any investment opportunity that exceeds that level and rejects any investment opportunity below that level. Theoretically, the ROI thresh-old should be equal to the discount rate, both of which should represent the company's cost of securing capital. However, this is not a practical expectation since the ROI threshold may need to be adjusted higher for such purposes as accounting for a margin of error in the calculations, protecting against potential overlap, and recovering general marketing expenses. Companies may choose to set multiple ROI thresh-olds based on the level of risk anticipated for the marketing investment or based on strategic development stages.

DEFINING INCREMENTAL VALUE

Ideally, ROI calculations measure the incremental return generated by incremental marketing investment. Marketing investments can be broken down into very small incremental levels, from the addition of a marketing channel or offer to one more targeted prospect. Incremental return is subject to more discretion by the company, depending on the data available and the finance department's approach.

This impacts the way gross margin is measured Producing products and services requires a combination of fixed costs and variable costs. General Business expenses must also be allocated appropriately and covered within the cost of goods sold. Any incremental expenses specific to a sale are included in the gross margin calculation so that the return truly captures just profits (before deduct-ing the marketing investment).

POINT-OF-DECISION PERSPECTIVE

Marketing ROI is intended to help guide the best decisions for marketing investments. To drive the right decisions, the calculation of ROI will differ for strategic planning and performance measurement. Strategic planning occurs before a marketing investment and the performance measure occurs after changing the decision-making perspective.

To maintain the objective of maximizing profits, investments must be directed toward the best opportunities available at the time. This requires a point-of-decision perspective where the past investment decisions do not influence the investment decisions of the present. The marketing budget must constantly be allocated or reallocated to generate the best possible return.

The key distinction is that ROI projections in the planning stage can exclude previous investments to support the point-of-decision perspective. At the same time, ROI analyses for performance measurement should include all historical costs ensuring that each investment decision stands on its own merits.

It is possible that marketing initiatives already underway may lose funding using this approach. In certain situations, market conditions change the initial assumptions, additional requirements are identified, or better investment opportunities come along. With a point-of-decision perspective, new investments are not made to justify previous investments. Poor investment decisions of the past may still be leveraged to provide profitable returns from future investments.

CHAPTER 3

MARKETING ROI IS DIFFERENT

ROI is a measure used by a company's financial managers to guide the company's major investment decisions. To understand how marketing ROI is different from ROI analyses completed in other business areas, it makes sense to look at capital investments where ROI is a standard part of the decision-making process. For example, a financial manager may evaluate an expansion opportunity for a business that requires new machinery. Several machinery pieces may be considered, each at different price points with different operating and maintenance expenses and different capabilities. All of the future incremental profits and expenses will be discounted to calculate a net present value. The projected net returns will be compared to the investments, and the best ROI that meets the company's minimum ROI (hurdle rate) and strategic goals will be selected. In another example, the ROI may be used to assess new technology for Customer Relationship Management (CRM).

The expenses to install and operate the CRM system would be compared to the expected returns generated from changes to customer-retention rates, customer profitability, productivity gains, and customer service savings. The projected ROI could be used to justify an investment and select the best choice.

Marketing investments are prioritized and selected much differently from capital investments, requiring a different approach to ROI analysis and more creative use of the ROI calculation.

First of all, the number of marketing investments, the frequency of investments, and the relatively small increments in which investments can be made create an incredible number of decision-making possibilities, while capital investments are typically limited to infrequent, large-scale investments. The assumptions that go into marketing ROI measurements are subject to change regularly as competition, customer needs, and marketing channel expenses change. Based on this, marketing ROI measurements must be

- Flexible
- Dynamic
- Focused on each incremental investment

Marketing Has Greater Flexibility

Marketing is very scalable compared to capital investments where, for example, it is unlikely that an investment will be made in 50 percent of the needed machinery or CRM system. Marketers must consistently decide how much advertising is required, how many contacts to reach with direct marketing, how frequently customers should be marketed to, and the ideal customer modeling point. Each marketing campaign can be composed of a wide range of channel combinations, packaged with a wide range of offer values, scaled to a wide range of prospect populations, and viable at a wide range of investment levels. Marketing investment decisions are more complex than deciding to invest or not invest and go beyond a decision to select the best investment choice from a pool of alternatives.

CHAPTER 4

MORE MEASURABLE THAN EVER

Marketing, no matter what practitioners thought in the past, is more science than art. It is no longer necessary to rely on a hunch, hope, mythology, experience, creative breakthroughs, and divine illumination. The data and tools currently exist to dramatically improve a company's marketing programs for new and established products and services. All that's required is the will to use them.

Marketing is becoming more measurable based on the advancements of technology and the growth in electronic marketing channels such as e-mail marketing and Web advertising. Direct marketing has a history of being fairly measurable, while mass advertising has been more challenging to measure. Test marketing has been a primary measure for gauging the impact of marketing and advertising by using controlled comparisons between segments of the market exposed to the marketing to those not exposed. Marketing measurements are based on a combination of actual behaviors, quantitative testing, and educated assumptions.

Marketing contained entirely on the Internet is among the easiest to track. Not only can results be measured in terms of sales but also in the interim behaviors such as open rate of E-mail, click-stream patterns of Web pages viewed, and repeat visits. The abundance of data becomes as much a challenge as it is a benefit. With the proper data in hand, it's much easier in online marketing to understand both customer's and prospects' behaviors and, in real-time, make strategic decisions for modifying the marketing to improve results.

The reality is that most marketing initiatives are multichannel, combining Internet marketing with traditional marketing and retail channels. Customers want relationships where multiple channels can be used throughout the communication and transaction experience. This significantly adds to the tracking complexity and requires integrating information from many sources to provide a comprehensive picture at a campaign or customer level. The key is to gain access to the data, test assumptions, understand the limitations of the information available, and make constant improvements in the decision-making process.

The trend of measurement capabilities is likely to further increase over time. Available technology can take current individual exposure to advertising and individual behaviors within existing channels much further than it is today. These new capabilities questions arise as to both the economic feasibility of implementation and individual privacy's social issues.

Here are some ways that marketing measurements are being improved or could potentially become available in the marketplace in the future, based on the level of customer support, industry support, and industry's ability to profit from offering additional measurement services.

- Advanced enterprise technology for enterprise resource planning (ERP) and CRM initiatives offer data flow to and from the many customer sales and marketing channels, which allows for improved measurements and integrated transaction information.

- Modeling for targeting high-value customers often contains predictive information on customer lifetime value, which helps improve ROI measures.

- Retail data is getting more sophisticated and more comprehensive.

- Mass media channels, such as television advertising, have been among the most difficult to measure. Cable TV companies are upgrading the wired connection between the house and the distribution point to allow for two-way communications. Technology can be implemented to identify the viewership of advertisements to the household level.

- Radio will be approaching a similar level of measurability if Inter-net radio or satellite subscription radio increases and more Internet-enabled entertainment appliances are introduced. Individuals currently can personalize their radio station programming through solutions such as MSN Entertainment or Yahoo!'s Launch.com. So not only could there be measurements of advertisements delivered at a household level, but also at the listener level as each household member gains the ability to personalize their advertising preferences as well as their listening preferences.

- Advertising on mobile devices and interactive cell phone technology will begin to accelerate, offering the same measurement and response tracking capabilities as the Internet.

- Taking the concept of mobile device tracking to an extreme, cell phone technology will eventually be capable of determining your exact physical location through Global

Positioning Systems (GPS). Privacy issues aside for the moment, this technology could be evolved to the point where an individual's exposure to outdoor ads and retail visits could be tracked based on knowing the person's physical location.

TECHNOLOGY SIMPLIFIES THE MEASURES

Determining ROI, incremental customer value, and profit optimization requires aggregating lots of data, modeling the information, and running calculations. This has traditionally required the support of statistical modeling experts who would spend weeks running analyses that may or may not meet the marketers' needs and would often require more time for additional analysis. Technology is placing more of the data analysis and modeling capabilities into the hands of the end-users. Data queries can be run in real-time, and any additional analysis that is needed can be completed instantly, greatly reducing cost and turn-around time. Marketers do not need to be experts in modeling, financial analysis, or even basic math if the right tools and training are provided.

Technology has advanced in campaign management, business intelligence, executive reporting, and sales force automation.

Other companies such as Marketswitch (mar ketswitch.com) offer specific marketing functionality such as profit and ROI optimization to support the selection of target customers, offers, and channels. Campaign management tools, both stand-alone and incorporated into CRM systems, are becoming more robust as tools to support marketers and provide executives with better insight into marketing performance.

CHAPTER 5

MARKETING ROI PROCESS

Let's take a look at what the entire marketing ROI process would encompass in an ideal world. The concepts presented in the remainder of this book may not fit every company nor be easily implemented into every corporate environment. If you can understand the key principles and the potential value, you should determine the best way to adapt the concepts into your environment.

As a brief preview of what will be presented, let's walk through the process at a very high level. The marketing ROI process is implemented at the campaign, customer, and corporate level to maximize company profits. Marketing ROI will be used to plan campaigns to run projections that help guide marketing strategy development. The campaigns will be implemented, and the results tracked. These results will be used to complete the ROI analysis that then serves as input into the marketing strategy for modifications and new developments (see Figure 5.1). Additional profits can be gained by looking beyond performance at the individual campaign level. Customer profitability will be maximized by measuring the ROI of several combinations of marketing campaigns delivered to the customer. The ROI projections for each possible marketing investment will be captured and subsequently prioritized for budget allocation at the corporate level.

- A standardized ROI formula will be used as the primary marketing measure. All marketing investment oppor-

tunities could then be easily compared and prioritized.
- An ROI threshold will be established by the financial organization, and management will generally fund the optimal mix of marketing opportunities that could exceed the ROI threshold.
- Budget allocation will be based on maximizing corporate profits with an appropriate balance between short-term and long-term profits. Marketing investments will be managed like an investment portfolio, which has risk diversification factored into the planning for profit optimization. A portion of the budget will be set aside for development and emerging strategies to support innovation and allow time for performance improvement.
- Marketing activities will be designed, measured, and managed to maximize customer profitability, which will maximize corporate profitability.
- The expense of measuring ROI and customer value will be kept cost-effective by using benchmark studies, modeling, and research studies.
- Complex analysis and ROI calculations will either be automated or performed by analytical experts to keep marketers focused on their

CHAPTER 6

MEASURING RETURN ON INVESTMENT

Marketing ROI should be used by marketing managers to compare and prioritize investment opportunities in the planning stage and to measure the actual performance relative to expectations in the analysis stage. It is a powerful financial tool that can guide strategies and investments toward greater profits for a company. Misunderstanding or misapplying the ROI formula creates plenty of room for error. Data quality and availability will be challenging enough, so every effort should be made to ensure the calculation is accurate. Knowing the intricacies of the formula, as presented here, will certainly help.

The bottom line is that ROI is a financial measure based on using clearly defined pieces of information. The "return" represents the financial gain beyond the initial investment. The "investment" is the total of all the expenses put at risk to generate the return. In general, each marketing investment is expected to contribute to profits as customers are influenced to purchase more. You want to earn all of your investment back and have extra profits since that is the company's primary goal. ROI is presented as a percentage, calculated by dividing the return by the investment.

The ROI value will be a positive percentage, a negative percentage, or zero. A positive ROI indicates you've earned more than enough prof-its to cover your investment. If the ROI is negative, you've lost money. Zero ROI is your income-based breakeven point. The ROI value will generally be measured against company objectives or used compared to other ROI values for decision making.

Calculating the Investment

When using ROI to guide decisions toward greater profitability, investment is defined as "the expense at risk." It does not include expenses related to delivering sales, which are factored into the gross margin. An expense belongs under investment if it is incurred when absolutely no sales are generated. Those expenses related directly to sales are deducted from the gross margin calculation and are not included in the investment. Marketing expenses such as the development and implementation of advertising, direct mail, or point-of-purchase promotion may have costs identified as of the investment.

Investment = NPV of the sum of all at-risk marketing expenses

This is equal to the NPV of:

Variable expenses (mass media, direct to consumer, sales support material)

- Marketing expense at risk
- Plus long-term expense commitments
- Plus staff resources required for development and implementation (sales, marketing, advertising, research, customer contact channels)
- Plus allocations of multicampaign investments (not to be included in projections for planning, strictly for post-implementation analysis)

The up-front and variable expenses may include the following:

- Creative development of marketing and advertising promotions
- Production and printing of materials
- Incremental distribution channel expenses
- Media and delivery expense
- Marketing lists
- The cost of promotional giveaways that are not sales-driven
- Database and system development to support the specific marketing campaign
- Research directly related to a specific campaign
- External strategic planning resources for the campaign
- Cost for staff time for marketing, sales, project management, executive and administrative support (if tracked as part of the investment, these expenses should not be included as overhead in Cost of Goods Sold)
- Channel promotions and preparation (i.e., training before the campaign start)
- The cost of inquiries or service through contact channels beyond sales processing (the investment may require an expense budget to handle the high-contact volume that does not convert to sales)
- Measurement systems and research studies
- Allocated expenses for general marketing support

Long-term expense commitments will apply only to select market-ing investment decisions such as a loyalty program or special media purchases that include a contractual commitment. When these expenses are included in the ROI calculation, all expected financial returns from these future expenses should also be included.

Challenges Associated with Investment Data

Marketing expenses that go into the investment figure are typically easy to predict. The challenges are primarily in keeping the investment values aligned with the point of decision. Expenses associated with higher-level investments that will be made regardless of the decision to proceed with the marketing initiative to be measured should not be included in that ROI for planning purposes. The approaches presented in Part III can be very effective in providing the insight necessary to make the most profitable decisions.

Investment Data

The investment is typically easy to estimate before committing to the marketing initiative accurately. The required data will come from:

- Budget projections
- Actual expenses
- Expense allocation models

Recovering Development Costs

Creating a new marketing initiative or adapting an initiative for a new channel or strategy will require an up-front cost for development.

The cost of this development certainly must be part of the investment decision. More elaborate and expensive campaigns should have higher expectations for profit returns to achieve comparable ROI. In some cases, the development cost is initially associated with a small-scale market test, and the ROI measure must be viewed at the level of a large-scale rollout. In other cases, the initial marketing channel's high-development cost is then leveraged for lower-cost development in other channels, or it is reused for future marketing investments over a long period.

The ROI analysis must be adjusted to drive the right decisions. The goal is to apply the expense in a way that will be most appropriate. Here are three ways up-front costs can be treated based upon the situation and practices of the company.

1. **Absorb the development costs immediately.** Suppose the marketing campaign is a one-time campaign, or the expectation for future development investment is unknown. In that case, 100 percent of the development costs should be included in the ROI investment decision.

2. **Base the decision on the ROI projection for a full-scale rollout.** For marketing campaigns that will be test-marketed before rollout, the campaign should be developed with a full-scale ROI projection in mind. If the projected ROI for the full-scale program is expected to meet the company's ROI threshold, the decision will be to invest. Projecting all test marketing at a rollout level will leave many investment dollars unaccounted since not all campaigns test-marketed proceed to a rollout stage. This can be accounted for in two ways. First, allocate test marketing expenses as overhead or second, manage a portion of the budget for emerging campaigns where the ROI expectation is lower.

3. **Assess incremental and allocated investments.** Some development costs benefit multiple campaigns, such as purchasing a prospect mailing list or improving website functionality. This may be driven by one initial marketing initiative, even though the benefit

applies to many. The ideal approach is to assess the ROI of this special investment on its own—the incremental return generated from the incremental investment.

Calculating the ROI

The ROI calculation for marketing initiatives has to be as flexible and dynamic as marketing itself. You must calculate the ROI on a corporate aggregate marketing spend, as a whole. However, it's important to drill down further into ROI for incremental investments, which calculates additional returns/additional spend. You must also ask, "what is my expected return on just this incremental investment?"

Decision making doesn't just stop there. It would help if you looked at the ROI, based on an aggregate campaign. Independent of this analysis, answer the question, "do I invest in Campaign X and Campaign Y, or either X or Y?" For this reasoning, you must clearly define the formula and the elements that make up the formula.

When you're determining how to calculate marketing ROI, define the elements that make up the investment.

This is then divisible by your total investment. Some businesses use various elements for the total investment calculation, including the initial cost and long-term expense commitments and staff utilization, versus new hires (and other factors) calculated to the NPV (value of all future cash flows).

The marketing ROI benchmarks are the same as any fixed investment benchmark. Defining a benchmark is paramount to how a business will measure the success of their marketing strategy.

To determine if the marketing strategy is successful, the following is an ROI measurement process to consider:

- ROI benchmark
- Strategy/cost
- Execution
- Results
- Analysis of results
- Adjust strategy and assumptions
- Go back to the marketing ROI benchmark and determine what you might need to change.

Here are the best ways to increase marketing ROI:

BUILD AN INTEGRATED MARKETING COMMUNICATIONS CAMPAIGN

Today, because of the many diverse platforms available, there's no single marketing approach that will work better than building a successful integrated marketing communications campaign.

This traditional marketing method assures that your message is being delivered to your target audiences, regardless of how they interact with your brand, whether through advertising, social media marketing, public relations or digital marketing. It also offers you the ability to outline a core message and highlight its unique selling proposition to an identified target market, with a tailored message, through various mediums.

Having a strong integration between the tactics used to build brand awareness, nurture prospects and close sales is one of the best ways to increase marketing ROI.

MAKE DECISIONS BASED ON SALES IMPACT.

Give attention to the budget to make decisions that have a greater impact on sales and close rates. This begins by determining the marketing tactics, key messages and content that will best resonate with your target audience. Then, measure metrics comprising sales objectives, i.e., customer/member retention), along with business results that encompass market share and revenue.

MAXIMIZE CURRENT CUSTOMERS SPEND

It's easier and takes less time to maximize current customers' spend by building customer loyalty and improving customer experience. Continue to communicate to your customers with empathy and know how you are keeping them and employees safe by adhering to new health and safety protocols. Roll out messaging that addresses your audiences' concerns about safety, as well as new product and service offerings.

Improving customer loyalty is the easiest way to increase sales because those customers already know and trust you. Selling to current customers offers you an opportunity to cross-sell and upsell them on your other services—which will deliver excellent ROI.

Cross-selling and upselling are key. It's 5-25 times more expensive to acquire a new customer than retain an existing one. When you do retain a customer, they're more likely to spend extra and purchase more frequently. You are also 60-70% likely to sell to an existing customer, compared to the 5-20% likelihood of selling to a new prospect. If your business isn't cross-selling and upselling, you're not maximizing ROI.

ALIGN SALES AND MARKETING ACTIVITIES WITH SMART DATA

Sales and marketing departments need to align their marketing efforts to grow their business and build an audience. This includes having a strong content marketing strategy and supporting and engaging customers with great content. This can range from blog posts to videos.

To achieve that, smart data is key. Businesses that utilize smart data in their content marketing effort will drive higher sales and marketing ROI. Content marketing costs 62% less than traditional marketing and generates about three times as many leads. To boot, conversion rates are nearly six times higher for content marketing adopters than non-adopters.

INCORPORATE ROI INTO YOUR MARKETING PLAN

When building your yearly marketing plan, including ROI. In my blog on marketing planning and creating a marketing budget to drive growth, I shared that the real secret to getting your marketing budget passed is to start with ROI and answer, "Why should this money be spent on marketing, as opposed to in other departments?" This could be a challenge for many marketers, as the Nielsen study reported.

CHAPTER 7

ADOPTING THE MARKETING ROI PROCESS

A company exists to maximize profits. Companies deliver many other great outcomes, but for the most part, all the work that is done to create superior products and services and expand the base of satisfied customers at the lowest expense are ultimately measured by how well the company increases profits. The ROI calculation foundation was laid out to prepare you to collect and organize the right data for more accurate use. Now it is time to take this information and put it to work. In this Part, the focus becomes much more strategic. Specific responsibilities are provided to manage profitability at the corporate, customer, and campaign level and steps are outlined to customize and apply the marketing ROI process effectively.

Even at this point, it is safe to assume that not everyone is comfortable with the intense focus on profits. You don't like to think that you are in business just for the money. Your company generates great products and services that people love and need. You invest heavily in employee satisfaction or product quality because that leads to high levels of customer satisfaction. You might even have concerns that if you focus on profits, eventually neither employees nor customers will be satisfied.

This emphasis on maximizing profits is not at all in contradiction with customer or employee satisfaction. First of all, the tools and concepts are geared toward improving long-term profits for the company while also managing short-term profit goals. Company management is well aware that it is impossible to lose sight of either employee or customer satisfaction and still expect to remain profitable in the long run.

The goal is to effectively prioritize your marketing investments so that the finite budget you have to work with is directed toward generating the greatest return. Applying the marketing ROI process can create a distinct competitive advantage, allowing you to make smarter decisions on whom to target, how to reach them, and how much to invest. The more the competition wastes their marketing budget on unprofitable efforts, the less share of the market they can earn.

What does increasing corporate profits do for you? By applying these processes, you should end up with benefits such as more customers, better customers, lower costs per sale, stronger customer relationships, and increased customer loyalty—all because you focus your marketing where it has the greatest impact. It would help if you still had great business and marketing strategies, but you are now more equipped to develop, measure, and refine those strategies.

There is an opportunity for customer and employee satisfaction to benefit, as well. Generating the best return on your marketing investment provides more financial resources to reinvest in such ways that will increase customer satisfaction and employee satisfaction. It increases the stability of the company and strengthens the company's viability during uncertain economic times. Ultimately, it should fatten the bonus checks for employees and dividend checks for stockholders, both of whom want to be rewarded for making smart investment decisions of their own.

Putting Marketing ROI to Work

So are you ready to champion the marketing ROI revolution for your company? In so many areas within an organization, simple ROI tools, and an increased focus on ROI can contribute to company profits. CEOs and senior marketing executives can shift from running endless iterations within the budgeting process to a streamlined marketing investment prioritization process. Market-ing managers can improve their campaign strategies with increased intelligence and measures. Managers of marketing divisions can play a stronger role in aligning the optimal series of campaigns and programs targeted over a customer lifetime.

The next three chapters will apply marketing ROI to improve corporate-level profitability, customer profitability, and campaign profitability. Before getting into those chapters, the following overview will put each level of the company's key responsibilities into context. Not all aspects of the marketing ROI process need to be adopted at once or in a specific order. And even though the executives at the corporate level should be setting key financial parameters, there are ways to work around this if necessary. If you are going to be the marketing ROI champion for your company, go in with the mindset that you'll be able to benefit from new insights, regardless of how widespread the marketing ROI process is adopted. You can find areas within your responsibilities to achieve initial success and then motivate others to expand upon that success.

Corporate-Level Responsibilities

Ultimately, the most significant decision the executive team needs to make is to what degree the company will adopt marketing ROI to do business. If the company is prepared to move forward with the marketing ROI process fully, then top marketing executives, along with the company's financial executives, have the following responsibilities:

- Establish the standard measure of ROI to be used consistently across the organization.
- Set a minimum ROI threshold above which all marketing activities can be funded.
- Where applicable, conduct research to establish standard values for ROI calculations to capture the full future impact on profits or expenses.
- Use the marketing ROI process to set and adjust marketing division and program budgets.
- Align compensation and recognition with the corporate goal to maximize marketing ROI. Mobilization of the organization is just as important as building the tools and capabilities.
- Ensure that the company has access to financing to fund marketing activities that exceed the minimum ROI threshold.
- Monitor and modify the process as needed.

The ROI formula can empower marketing staff when standards are in place for creating projections and making decisions. Suppose the company is willing to begin implementing the marketing ROI process at a campaign or customer level only and not at the corporate level. In that case, the corporate executives should at least set the minimum ROI threshold that the company expects from its investments. Marketers can judge on their own that a negative ROI is not good but cannot do much to evaluate a positive ROI without having a threshold set by the company. Even choosing a better investment out of two campaigns requires an ROI threshold to make a decision. For example, how could a marketer determine if a program generating 15 percent ROI for a total of $1 million in gross margin is better than a program generating 30 percent for a total of $500,000 in gross margin? The threshold also establishes a reference point for a marketing organization with promising new opportunities to request additional budget.

Division-Level Responsibilities

The division is defined, for our purposes, as the organization that has control over the majority of marketing activities for a specific set of customers and can manage customer profitability. In some companies, this may be a distinct business unit or line of business. In other companies, the organizational structure is set more by product line or functional area than by customer segment. For the latter type of companies, the marketing ROI process and tools can still work very effectively; how-ever, certain strategic planning will need to be made by the cross-division team that can represent a complete view of the overall marketing relationship with the customer segment.

Division management should assume the following responsibilities when implementing the marketing ROI process for profit maximization:

-
- Measure multiple levels of ROI performance to capture the value of the independent campaigns, incremental options,

MARKETING: RETURN ON INVESTMENT

and aggregated campaigns.
- Establish a methodology to measure mass marketing and investments, contributing to a broad number of campaigns.
- Establish a Customer Pathing process for strategically managing marketing efforts at a higher level for maximum profits.
- Manage budgets dynamically to maximize ROI at the corporate level.
- Support marketing ROI measures with research, development, and benchmarking.
- Evaluate and implement systems to track and manage customer profitability.

Campaign-Level Responsibilities

The marketing managers responsible for developing and managing campaigns and promotions can use the marketing ROI process in many ways for both measuring and planning. Responsibilities at this level are as follows:
- Develop marketing ROI tools such as investment limits and allowable marketing charts for easy reference as a checkpoint in the initial planning stage.
- Streamline campaign innovation by applying ROI projections to compare potential campaigns against performance requirements.
- Design market tests to effectively maximize learning and effectively project profitability of large-scale rollouts.
- Strategically identify the most profitable campaign marketing mix by applying marketing ROI principles within marketing channel optimization modeling.
- Apply marketing ROI principles for results measurements to maximize campaign profitability.
- Strategically set the most profitable target market profile by applying marketing ROI principles within targeting and marketing mix optimization modeling.

- Coordinate Customer Pathing based on division-level strategies.

The True View of Marketing ROI

It is common practice in marketing organizations to test multiple campaigns and compare the ROI generated from each. The incremental marketing ROI measure presented here is a more sophisticated process for measuring marketing programs' ROI. Briefly introduced in the initial chapters of this book, this new process's general concept is to break down each incremental investment opportunity and measure ROI at that level. This is perhaps one of the simplest and most significant advances in measurements that a company can choose to adopt. It offers a great opportunity to see an immediate impact on corporate profits by making only slight shifts from the current standard measurements of marketing programs. This measure can be applied at the campaign, customer, and corporate levels. Marketing results and decisions can be surprisingly different using this very simple enhancement for measuring ROI.

Examples of Incremental Measures

As the following examples show, the typical process of testing campaign variations and selecting a campaign based on the total ROI measured for each can lead to lost profits. These two examples consist of a very basic comparison between a standard direct-mail campaign and the same campaign with a bonus offer.

A direct-mail campaign is tested with and without a financial offer. Assume that the campaign without the financial offer has been the proven performer, achieving a return on investment that exceeds the company's minimum ROI threshold of 20 percent. The marketer tests the same direct-mail campaign with and without a $25 offer paid out for each new sale. The market test is done with a sample from the prospect base, and the decision must be based on the best campaign to reach the total base of 500,000 prospects.

The incremental customer value (ICV) is assumed to remain consistent between the two campaigns to simplify the example. A promotional offer such as this would likely attract a different type of customer with a different value than the standard direct-mail campaign, but that will not be considered at this point. As a note, the ICV here represents the net present value of current and future gross margin.

What are some observations that a marketer would make on these projections?

- The sales conversion rate increases 60 percent by adding the $25 offer, which is quite significant. Companies relying on the sales conversion rate (also referred to as the response rate in some industries) would use this as the key measure for the rollout decision.
- The marketing investment would need to increase significantly since the $25 offer must be paid out on all sales.
- Even with the significant jump in the total budget, the cost per sale will increase by only a very small amount, roughly 5.6 percent.
- The offer can bring in $225,000 of additional profit from the same population of 500,000 consumers.
- The ROI of the direct mail with the offer is lower than the direct mail without the offer; however, at an ROI of 22.4 percent, it does exceed the 20 percent minimum ROI threshold set by the company.

What decision should a marketer make? Companies that are not yet using ROI thresholds might choose based on the cost-per-sale value, which shows that the addition of the $25 offer will not beat the cost per sale of the standard direct-mail package. Without an ROI analysis, however, there is no accurate way to judge if a 5.6 percent increase in cost per sale is worth the additional profit generated. Had the ICV varied between campaign responders, an analysis based on cost per sale would have been even less valid. A cost-per-sale comparison has little meaning when the sale value is different between the two campaigns being compared.

CHAPTER 8

MANAGING CORPORATE-LEVEL PROFITABILITY

Company executives are constantly working to maximize their profits while keeping the business on course for overall success and viability. Each company has its process for allocating budgets to various divisions within the marketing organization. The intention, of course, is to place budgets where there is the greatest profit potential.

Company profits can be maximized by funding all marketing programs that can generate an acceptable return on investment as defined by its performance goals and ability to fund investments. In a corporate environment where the total marketing budget has a fixed dollar limit, profits can be maximized by prioritizing funds into the ROI rank-ordered list of marketing investments and selecting the top performers.

The budgeting process is not the only deterrent to making the right investments in marketing. There is no doubt that if you are in a mid-size or larger corporation, you have gone through midyear budget cuts on more than a few occasions. This process is typically more chaotic than the initial budgeting process. Profit pressures usually drive bud-get cuts, yet the cuts work against optimizing profits. The entire process of allocating and reallocating budgets unnecessarily burns up marketers' time and energy that should be directed toward generating results.

The marketing ROI process is an opportunity to establish a more effective process for budgeting and adjusting marketing investments. It should optimize profits at a point in time and set off the triggers that indicate when an adjustment to the budget is needed. The process will require work to adopt fully but should ultimately simplify the ongoing process.

Executive Responsibilities

As a recap, here are the responsibilities at the corporate level as presented in the previous chapter:

- Establish the standard measure of ROI to be used consistently across the organization.
- Set a minimum ROI threshold above which all marketing activities can be funded.
- Where applicable, conduct research to establish standard values for ROI calculations to capture the full future impact on profits or expenses.
- Use the marketing ROI process to set and adjust division and program budgets.
- Align compensation and recognition with the corporate goal to maximize marketing ROI. Mobilization of the organization is just as important as building the tools and capabilities.
- Ensure that the company has access to financing to fund marketing activities that exceed the minimum ROI threshold.
- Monitor and modify the process as needed.
- The core principle behind ROI is as simple as can be:
- Investment is the total of all expenses that are put at risk.
- Net profit is all of the financial gain (or loss) resulting from that investment.

- Return is the difference between the two.
- ROI is the return as a percent of the investment.

The only real complexity that comes into the ROI measure is what gets counted within the investment and gross margin values and how those input variables are calculated. Establishing standards is necessary to simplify the use of ROI measurements.

Standardizing the ROI Formula

Clear standards must be established for calculating ROI across an entire corporation. The return on investment calculation provides a numeric value used as a measure or projection of performance. That value can have lots of meaning when put in the context of other ROI values. Measuring customer and campaign profitability may have unique nuances for some companies, which must be addressed at a high level in the corporation to maintain the consistency necessary for accurate comparisons. If a company embarks on profit optimization using the marketing ROI process, it must ensure strict adherence to a standard ROI formula set at the corporate level.

Standardization also minimizes the fudge factor that gets incorporated into the reporting of results to management. Employees, consultants, and agencies are motivated to make performance measures look as good as possible. The measurement of a marketing program's ROI is often enhanced by identifying additional value or using alternative assumptions. Completeness and consistency go a long way in providing valuable intelligence in measures and decision making.

Many issues will arise when setting the parameters of the ROI formula. Choices to include or exclude certain input variables will make the results and projections from some divisions and campaigns appear more favorable and others less favorable. This process will certainly be a catalyst for discussion and debate in those cases and should be handled carefully to ensure all management and employees buy into the process.

As mentioned previously, it is very important to differentiate the ROI formula for planning strategies and measuring performance. To maximize profits, you want to guide the marketing investment decisions, which typically happens at the planning stage. When goals and compensation are aligned with maximizing corporate profits, ROI measures of performance will also be very important.

The key difference to keep in mind is that the ROI calculation for measuring performance should consider all related expenses past and present as the investment. In contrast, the ROI calculation for planning should consider only investments that have yet to be made relative to other investments that could be made with the same budget.

Decisions that need to be made to establish the ROI formula for planning include:

- **Period.** The period determines which future profits and expenses get included in the calculations.
- **Incremental customer value.** Measuring the average expected incremental customer value must be done with consistency. The measurement process must establish guidelines for estimating revenue, Cost of Goods Sold (COGS), incremental savings, and ongoing customer maintenance. Determining if the cost of goods will incorporate fully-loaded costs or purely incremental costs will be an important decision that must come from the

executive level.

- **Discount rate.** The discount rate(s) for adjusting future profits and expenses into net present value must be standardized at the corporate level. It is also important to designate whether the NPV applies on an annual basis, monthly basis, or some other period.
- **Referral value.** The value associated with customer referrals and the incidence of referrals from new customers and influencers must have established procedures for being included in the ROI calculation.
- **Expense allocation.** For performance measurement using ROI, all expenses that contribute to generating returns and are not included in the CGS should be allocated to align with decision-making, not overlap, and cover 100 percent of these shared-benefit expenses.
- **Investment.** The investment is defined as the total expenses "at risk." This includes any new expense that results from the decision to invest, and that will be incurred independent of generating any sales. If the expense is directly related to the sale, it is considered a cost of goods and is deducted when calculating the gross margin.
- **Residual value view.** Guidelines must be established for capturing the residual value of marketing investment on future marketing efforts, including the impact on results from marketing, the value chain, and the use of market intelligence. This is not a component of the ROI equation but must be shown in a separate view and considered during the prioritization of marketing investments.

Here are some general guidelines for establishing standards for each of the above input variables included in the ROI equation.

PERIOD

The period in which the costs and profits should be captured will typically fall in the range of three to six years. The goal is to allow enough time to capture an accurate view of the stream of profits and expenses that flow from the investment included in the ROI equation. A period that is too short may eliminate marketing programs that have significant growth in value over time. A period that is too long may be difficult to measure and, even with adjustments, will be at risk for uncontrollable changes that impact future value.

The time is partially influenced by the discount rate, making each successive period worthless in net present value. As this diminishes, there is less need to include future value. The higher the discount rate used, the shorter the time that needs to be used.

The considerations that can help determine the appropriate period to use as the standard include:

- What is a typical period over which a marketing activity has an impact? The period does not need to extend past the point where most of the value and costs are accurately captured.

- What degree of uncertainty is there in future value? Some degree of risk can be accounted for in the discount rate. Still, the period can also be used to focus the measurements on financials within a period where there is reasonable confidence.

- What are the short-term priorities for profits? Companies that place greater importance on short-term profits can either standardize on a short period or increase the discount rate each year, impacting diminishing returns.

There is the length of time that must be standardized and the duration of a single period. It is easiest to discount the value of money every year, but for businesses that are highly dependent on cash flow in the near term, it may make sense to use quarterly or monthly increments. This would provide better comparisons of marketing investments that generate faster returns when cash flow might make the difference in a company's ability to survive or thrive.

Incremental Customer Value

The challenge with incorporating customer value into the ROI calculation is collecting enough information to project future value with reasonable confidence. Incremental customer value is a critical component in the ROI measure, so assumptions must be made based on short-term data and validated.

There are two primary approaches to establishing an incremental customer value (ICV) figure used in ROI calculations—assess historical purchase behaviors or estimate anticipated purchase behaviors. Viewing historical patterns of customer value should be done as a benchmark whenever possible. When using strictly historical values to establish ICV, it is important to measure this for different customer segments so those values can be associated with marketing targeted to those different customer segments.

Companies entering new markets and do not have a comparable customer segment to develop a historical view, or those with solid reasoning that the future value will be much different from the past will need to create estimated values based on anticipated behaviors. In many cases, the historical view is the basis of the estimate, and it is then adjusted to reflect a campaign designed to change specific behaviors.

Another method for establishing assumptions for ICV is to research with customers of competitors or comparable companies to identify benchmark measurements. This needs to be done carefully to identify the specific factors driving the ultimate value so that the assumptions can be relied upon. For example, measuring the average value of a competitor's customer and estimating how much of that competitor's share your marketing efforts can capture is a sound process. However, your value from that same customer may be much different based on a difference, such as a customer service, which may be the primary driver of long-term value.

Each marketing campaign or the program will generate sales from different types of customers. Using a general ICV, or even the average ICV for the segment of customers targeted will neglect the impact of that specific marketing activity (at least until the actual ICV is tracked over a long period). To more accurately capture the ICV for each marketing activity, the company can determine which new customers' short-term behaviors predict long-term behaviors and lifetime value. Short-term behaviors such as lower customer satisfaction ratings with the initial transaction may indicate higher customer defection or lower future profits. Or the monetary value or type of product/service purchased in the initial transaction may be an initial indicator of future purchases. Monitoring these behaviors can establish ICV and be used as part of the

Customer Pathing process to guide strategies for the next set of marketing efforts.

Technology that can track customer behaviors and modeling programs that can predict future value makes it easier to establish incremental customer value standards. It is important to remember that making decisions based on any quality information is generally better than making assumptions and decisions with no information in this or other areas.

To align measurements with decision making, there are several adjustments to ICV that can be factored in where appropriate. These include:

- **Price variations.** Frederick Reichheld indicates in his book The Loyalty Effect that loyal customers will often pay premium prices, which increases customer value. Typically the price premiums come from reduced use of discounts and promotions. Adjustments should be made when the marketing strategy is geared toward increasing loyalty, and there is the opportunity to realize price premiums.

- **Cost of goods variations.** The marketing ROI process is based on comparing incremental marketing investments to incremental returns. As sales volume increases, the cost of goods or fulfillment costs will tend to decrease. If the decrease in costs is significant, it represents additional profit per sale, reflected in the ICV. Determining which sales are the base volume and which are considered incremental may be complex; the key is to align the measure with the decision.

- **Overhead expenses.** Some costs, such as customer service, maybe captured as an average spread across all customers equally. Expenses that can be tracked to a customer level should be captured in the ICV to reflect better the actual profits generated.

Factors to consider when establishing incremental customer values include:

- **How effective can historical measures be in determining value?** Historical measures are reliable if consistent behaviors are predicted.

- **Can internal benchmarks be established for specific customer segments?** The company may want to offer internal benchmarks for various customer segments so that all marketing managers can use the same assumptions before making adjustments for anticipated value.

- **Are external benchmarks necessary?** Research to establish external benchmarks for various customer segments may be necessary to ensure that all marketing managers can use the same assumptions before making anticipated value adjustments.

- **What are the key behaviors that serve as indicators of ICV?** Identifying customers' key behaviors that occur shortly after the marketing activity can help assess the ICV of the converted customers.

- **Does the ICV represent the return on this investment?** Projections and measures must be monitored to ensure that only the portion of customer value that comes directly from the investment being measured is included in the ROI calculation.

DISCOUNT RATE

Marketers should not be too concerned with how the discount rate is set; leave this to the finance department. It is important to understand the fundamentals of the discount rate and how it can be used strategically to establish corporate standards for ROI calculations. From a financial standpoint, the discount rate is intended to reflect the rate at which additional capital can be raised for investment into the company—in this case, into marketing programs. The discount rate can be used to establish the priority of short-term profits relative to long-term profits.

Factors that can be used to determine the discount rate:

- At what rate of return could money receive this year be invested? The discount rate of 15 percent has become the de facto rate in calculating ROI since that is fairly close to an average long-term return within the stock market.

- At what rate could money be borrowed? Suppose a company could make marketing investments today that generate phenomenal profits in future years but not enough in the immediate years. In that case, the company should consider borrowing capital to cover the cash-flow gap.

- How does risk increase over time? Different discount rates can be used for each future period based on the risk of uncertainty.

REFERRAL VALUE

Referrals are a great source of new business. The ROI calculation should capture any additional net value generated from referrals traced back to the initial marketing investment. It's long been proven that highly satisfied customers tend to make referrals, and highly dissatisfied customers make even more negative referrals. Marketing investments that bring in new customers or change customer opinions will have a ripple effect on profits.

Referral profits can result from customers and influencers. Influencers are intermediaries such as experts, the media, or highly regarded individuals or entities that can help generate business by expressing their views and opinions. Marketing investments can impact influencers, leading to positive (or negative) growth in ROI. Influencers are defined here as unpaid individuals and entities to ensure no confusion with paid endorsements, a more traditional marketing tactic.

Referrals can sometimes be difficult to track and measure. The company should either set up tracking procedures, commission a study on actual customer behavior, or establish some benchmark values that can be used throughout the corporation.

EXPENSE ALLOCATIONS

To get an accurate and complete picture of the total investment responsible for generating the measured returns, it may be appropriate to allocate certain expenses across multiple marketing initiatives. Investments into marketing technology, staff, and even some forms of brand advertising are done to generate their ROI but, in many cases, will be dependent on additional future investments to capture that incremental value. Expense allocations must be structured to lead to optimal decisions since the process can backfire. The first step is to ensure that only pending investments be allocated to the ROI projections of individual campaigns. This allocation is part of the process of assessing the value of this investment.

The next step is to make sure all allocated expenses are not duplicated in the Cost of Goods Sold or anywhere else in the ROI equation. Expenses such as staff or technology are sometimes treated as fixed overhead costs and not viewed on an incremental basis.

Finally, the trick to effectively manage an allocation process is to take a series of iterations. Once an allocation process is established and costs are spread among several marketing campaigns, the change in ROI may lead to the decision that some campaigns are no longer profitable. When one campaign is dropped, it will change the allocation amounts for all other programs. This is where caution is necessary to avoid cancellation of marketing campaigns that may be incrementally profitable if other marketing initiatives can cover the expense.

Corporate-level decisions are necessary to establish standard allocation procedures.
- Which expenses get allocated and which belong in general overhead expenses? The general overhead expenses get captured in the cost of goods.
- What method of allocating expenses will be used? Expense allocations should be made very carefully to guide decisions toward the greatest profitability. Allocations should not unnecessarily burden marketing programs that will result in a loss of profits if rejected.

INVESTMENT AT RISK

The marketing expense for a specific campaign or marketing activity is usually known or is easy to estimate before deciding to move forward. It should be clear that all committed expenses must be included, and all expenses associated directly with each sale should not be included. Committed expenses packaged as PartPart of the planned marketing activity might include technology, training, incremental staff, or brand support. A good example of this would be a loyalty program where investments in many areas throughout the company would need to be committed before extending the offer to customers through marketing communications. The entire investment is at risk and should be compared to the total return that is expected.

RESIDUAL VALUE

The issues around capturing residual value in the ROI equation were presented in detail. Residual value can result from market-ing impacts such as increasing the customer base, changing perceptions of prospects, and collecting market intelligence to improve future targeting.

Typically, a greater investment is required to sell something to a new prospect than to sell the same thing to an existing customer. Based on this fact, there is value to having more customers, so the company is better positioned to generate more sales. This value would not be captured in the typical ROI measure of an acquisition campaign since, as defined, only the gross margin resulting from only the corresponding investment is considered. The future investment in the marketing campaign to the new customer is a separate decision with a separate ROI measure.

A similar gap is encountered when you consider that marketing campaigns generate sales and influence future marketing campaigns' impact on acquiring nonresponders. The campaign may increase awareness and understanding of the offer, change perceptions, and create interest that makes it easy to motivate purchase behavior in a future campaign. Conversely, the campaign's contact may also negatively impact if the prospect is being bombarded, which may deter future purchases. Either way, this marketing campaign is changing the potential return on future investments, which needs to be captured in the decision-making process.

Collecting market intelligence on prospects or customers can also have a tremendous value in terms of future marketing. Like the other residual value forms, this has no direct value until an additional investment is made.

No one wants to miss the opportunity to get credit for the value that has been created through his or her marketing campaigns. Many executives, marketing managers, agencies, and consultants have recognized this gap and have devised ways to establish values added to the ROI measurement. It would be great if it were that easy, but to maintain your ROI measures' integrity, the complexity around residual value must be considered.

SETTING THE ROI THRESHOLD

The ROI threshold guides marketing managers in deciding which campaigns and which incremental marketing investments should be pursued. This is the minimum ROI that the corporate executives expect from any marketing investment. It is not the average ROI that should be returned from all investments but a cutoff point where marketing programs below the threshold are rejected, except emerging marketing programs that are being tested and improved as discussed.

Ideally, a financially derived ROI threshold will be used to set the entire marketing budget for the corporation, but the reverse occurs in many cases. Companies establish arbitrary marketing budgets, which override the ROI threshold. The marketing initiatives that fall below the fixed budget (and are not funded) but are above an ROI threshold level that would be financially acceptable to the company represent lost profit opportunities. In addition to setting the initial budget, the ROI threshold should be used by marketing managers on an ongoing basis to request additional funding, serving as the point where proven marketing initiatives are funded under a blank check pol-icy. The company may have its way of calculating its minimum ROI expectations. Company goals for profits or profitability can determine it.

SETTING MARKETING BUDGETS

Setting marketing budgets begins at the corporate level and generally filters down so that marketing divisions then prioritize investments on a campaign level. The corporate executives deliver the budget with the expectations of achieving revenue and profit goals for the company.

The budgeting process is often based on benchmarks, such as the previous year's budget or a standard percentage of sales as a starting point. Financial projections are then run to determine how funds should be adjusted from previous benchmarks. At AT&T in the early 1990s, the process began with a starting budget and the assumption that budgets would be similar to the previous year. The process then involved running views of how much profit and revenue could be generated with that budget amount. Those views were then revised repeatedly at many different funding amounts for three months, and then the numbers were set. In the next quarter, the process was repeated in a fire drill series intended to cut that very same budget.

. The following steps should be taken to create a budgeting process designed to maximize profits.

- Establish standards for ROI measurement as outlined above so that projections are prepared consistently.
- Either select each incremental marketing investment that

exceeds the ROI threshold or ranks all incremental marketing investment opportunities and fund the top opportunities until the budget is depleted.

- Structure the company's investment portfolio to manage marketing programs in four categories: reliable investments, high-potential investments, emerging investments, and innovation investments. As explained, ROI thresholds and specific criteria for each category must be established.

MONITORING AND MODIFYING MARKETING BUDGETS

The responsibility for managing the marketing budget is ongoing. There must be a process established at the corporate level to streamline budget revisions throughout the year. To deliver on maximizing profits, adjustments must be made as the projections for marketing programs are replaced with actual measured results or improved assumptions. Those investments funding underperforming programs must be shifted to fund higher-performing programs.

Campaign management technology can play a significant part in both the initial and ongoing budget allocation processes. Through campaign management applications, executives can have access to marketing program results and projections. A custom-designed application can be developed to automatically rank programs based on projected ROI, track performance relative to projections, and alert management when a reallocation is necessary.

Just as budgets between marketing divisions may need adjustments based on actual performance, the ROI threshold may need to be adjusted throughout the year. Keep in mind that the ROI threshold is where marketing investments that exceed the threshold are to be made. Overall, suppose the marketing performance is running below projections, and there are no higher performing marketing programs into which investment can be shifted. In that case, it may be necessary to lower the ROI threshold temporarily. This must be done very carefully and with a strategic plan in mind. Lowering the threshold will allow additional profits to come in a while, not fully meeting the company's financial requirements (especially if the ROI threshold was properly set based on the cost of borrowing capital). Funding this increased marketing activity allows a period to improve the profitability of those programs.

Changes to the ROI threshold should not be confused with changes to goals for marketing. Marketing personnel should be motivated to achieve the highest level of ROI possible. However, the ROI threshold should be set as low as possible so that every marketing investment that can generate an acceptable return is funded.

ALIGNING PERFORMANCE REWARDS

New procedures for maximizing profits can have tremendous value to the corporation—but only if there are the proper motivation and mobilization of management and staff at every level within the marketing and sales organization.

The reality is that adopting the recommendations presented here must be supported by a shift in mindset from everyone from the marketers to the executives. Marketers are not motivated to openly admit when their ROI performance falls below a corporate threshold or to sacrifice their program results to help another marketer's results under a Customer Pathing strategy.

MODIFYING THE ROI THRESHOLD

The ROI threshold sets the minimum ROI to justify an investment. Market testing is being done to identify new campaigns that can exceed a successful campaign's performance already in place. The ROI threshold that must be achieved is that of the existing campaign. The investment limits and allowable marketing charts can be developed by substituting the existing campaign's ROI in place of the corporate ROI threshold. This sets a minimum level that is required for new campaigns to be considered successful.

CAMPAIGN INNOVATION AND SCREENING

Marketing allowable, investment limits, and planning charts provide quick reference during the development of new campaign strategies. They can also help marketers that are less comfortable with ROI calculations understand the correlation between different variables that go into marketing strategies and tactical plans. These tools are no substitute for using actual ROI projections, especially since the tools are based on the "break-even" levels to achieve minimum ROI while optimizing ROI for maximum profits.

New marketing strategies and campaign concepts are an essential part of remaining competitive and improving marketing profitability. ROI projections based on available assumptions are the first checkpoint to determine the viability of an investment. The next step is a market test to confirm assumptions with limited expenditures. Market tests are not always possible based on either a limitation of measurement capabilities or the need to take the chance on an immediate full-scale rollout. Standards should be set for how development and start-up costs should be allocated using the direction provided. New campaigns do not always achieve full potential in the first attempt, so a portion of the marketing budget should be set aside for emerging marketing investments that continue through the testing stage until achieving performance beyond the ROI threshold level.

The assumptions used in ROI projections for each campaign concept should reflect the customer behaviors that are likely for each specific campaign and not based on averages for variables such as customer value or sales conversion rates. For example, a campaign that incorporates strong viral marketing activity may be expected to generate above-average value from customer referrals. Or a campaign based on short-term price promotions may be expected to generate less long-term customer value than the average value per customer. Even if all campaigns target the same prospect base with the same product, adjusting the values to reflect the campaign's nature will result in more accurate projections and better investment decisions.

ROI PROJECTIONS

The basic ROI equation is used to calculate projections for each campaign concept. Assumptions will need to be based on the intelligence available. Each campaign concept will then have an estimated ROI to allow categorization ranging from high potential to small incremental potential. For campaigns where the assumptions are weak, consider running best-case and worst-case projections in addition to the most likely view.

In the planning phase, decisions are not based on ROI alone. Each company will use its method for prioritizing the campaigns to be tested. Here are some factors to consider in assessing which concepts to test:

- Which campaigns have the highest likelihood of exceeding the minimum ROI for rollout? Even if these do not have the highest ROI potential, those with a better chance of achieving incremental profits should be strongly considered.
- Which campaigns can potentially generate the highest ROI? If the concept is valid and the chance for success is reasonable, a big gain can be valuable.
- How much budget is available for testing? The budget limit may require a choice between testing several small concepts and testing very few high-cost concepts.
- How valid is the testing? Some marketing concepts will be more difficult to evaluate through a market test. Consider if other forms of research can help confirm or establish

assumptions for a rollout.
- How much can be learned within the market test? A well-designed market test can lead to results that provide insight across multiple concepts.
- What is the relative scale to which the campaigns can be launched? Campaigns that are expected to generate lower ROI (still above the threshold) but can scale to a larger size and generate more profits than other campaigns should be given strong consideration.

OFFER COMPARISON ANALYSIS

Marketing expenses directed to prospects are PartPart of the "investment" side of the ROI equation, while special offers paid out as PartPart of the sale shows up as a deduction on the "return" side. This creates an interesting dynamic that is worth presenting as PartPart of campaign strategy development.

CHAPTER 9

THE MEASUREMENT PROCESS

There's a saying in business that "you can't manage what you can't measure." The reality is that not everything is measurable, and some measurements are either inaccurate or misinterpreted.

Even So, measurements are critical to providing business intelligence and, when used in conjunction with the marketing ROI process presented here, can deliver more profits to the bottom line. Measurements that feed the ROI projections upon which marketing investments will be based are rarely perfect. Measurements need only have a reasonably high degree of accuracy and provide valid insight to value the decision-making process. A statement that best fits with the value of digging deeper through measurements and analysis is: "You can better manage what you can better understand."

Marketing measures are Part of the insight and intelligence that can connect marketing actions and customer behaviors to understanding and decision making.

To support better management and draw conclusions that support better understanding, measurements must have an acceptable level of accuracy, be complete, and be aligned with business goals. Poor quality data, flaws in the measurement formulas, or calculations can make otherwise good decisions into costly ones. Highly accurate measurements that are incorrectly assumed to be complete or do not effectively align with business goals can also lead to poor decisions. For example, companies that evaluate and choose marketing campaigns based totally on comparative cost-per-sale measures cannot capture differences in long-term customer value that is likely to exist. Ignoring long-term customer value leads to decisions that do not maximize profitability.

Similarly, decision making is sometimes based on measures assumed to correlate with profits, such as increased customer satisfaction or awareness. Most of the Time, exist-ing marketing measurements will be directionally in line with an ROI measure and lead to the correct decision—but is most of the time good enough when the potential exists to generate more profits from the same marketing budget?

The measurement process of data collection, assumptions, calculations, analysis, and interpretation requires continuous refinement and improvement. It is always important to understand which information can be fully trusted and which information has room for error or subjective interpretation. Where measurements are less reliable or possibly based on outdated data, the marketing team must determine whether gut instinct should override the projections or if further investments are justified to clarify the assumptions. Remember that gut instinct is typically based on a person's history with previous measures, analysis, and logic that is often beneficial in the decision process. Also, keep in mind that gut instinct incorporates personal preferences, background, and irrelevant history that may not be appropriate for making decisions.

INSIGHT FOR SMARTER DECISIONS

Measures are focused on past performance, which may be important to determine employee evaluations and compensation, but, for the most part will benefit the company most when used as insight into future decision making. As access to data is improved, and marketing becomes more real-time through the use of technology and automated processes,

measurements can be used to monitor performance and lead to faster decisions. Instead of waiting for results to be calculated several weeks later, the results-in-progress for a marketing campaign can be used to make strategy and tactical modifications during the campaign instead of just applying postcampaign analysis on future campaigns.

Not all marketing is measurable, and not all measurements are complete or precisely accurate. The challenge is to improve accuracy and make the best assumptions possible to enable better decision making. Improvements can come from better measurement practices, increased access to data, more powerful processing power and automated analysis capabilities, market research studies and predictive models that link known data points to future financial contributions. As marketing strategies evolve, especially concerning the recent migration toward CRM, the measurements will need to evolve.

Some basic principles to follow when planning out measurements:

- **Design measurements for optimal learning.** How will the information provide a greater understanding of the actions and behaviors generated by the marketing activity?

- **Invest in measurements intelligently.** How much value can be generated from the insight gained through the measurement research and analysis relative to the cost? If the measurement is strictly for evaluating past performance, how much value does that have to the company?

- Understand correlations between metrics that can be measured and the actual business goals behind the investment. How can you link metrics indicators with the goals through experimentation, validation research, or benchmark measures?

- **Avoid double counting results.** If a measurement analysis uncovers that a marketing investment has contributed to a financial return through some other sales channel, can you confirm that this return was not counted elsewhere? Is there a need to establish an offsetting deduction from another marketing investment originally assumed to generate that return?

- **Design the measurement to optimize future predictability.** Is the analysis objective enough that results are replicable and not overstated? Are there any hidden costs that must be factored into the next projection? Is there any value that should be attributed to a different marketing investment?

Using existing campaigns to predict future performance is effective when setting up a small-scale test market before launching the full marketing initiative on a large scale, or for ongoing marketing programs repeated based on trigger events such as customers moving households first-time buyers. The ROI measured on this completed marketing test becomes the basis for the ROI projection for identical marketing investments. Even a clear-cut direct measure of actual results is subject to error when used as a projection. The accuracy of the ROI projection is dependent on reaching a similar target market with the same offer, through the same channels. If the marketing initiative is not identical, adjustments must be made.

The effects of time on a repeated marketing effort can be difficult to predict. Seasonality and economic trends may be known or easily assumed and should require adjustments to the assumptions. Other time-oriented factors such as shifts in market needs, changes in competitive activity, unusual market conditions, or a company PR crisis can interfere with a market test or cause a marketing initiative to miss its target. Projections should always be based on the best estimate of the conditions expected for the period in which the income stream will occur.

Marketing ROI measures are dependent on the ability to track actual behaviors and to predict future behaviors. Companies that have a direct relationship with each customer have the advantage of connecting the campaign prospects with first-time buyers. Those without direct relationships, such as companies that rely on cash sales driven through retail outlets or intermediary companies that hold the customer relationship, are much more difficult to track. Controlled test markets can be used to compare the change in sales for markets with marketing treatment relative to those without the same marketing treatment.

Market research of customer attitudes or intentions may be justified in some situations; however, the ability to rely on customer perceptions to link actual actions with marketing campaigns must be based on proven methodologies. Other marketing activities that can assist in tracking include rebates directly to the company, product registrations, or service inquiries. These activities do not provide a complete picture but, with the appropriate analysis, can be used as a factor to estimate sales levels.

Predictive capabilities are necessary whenever customer value is partially based on a future stream of sales activities. Marketing ROI has the added benefit of guiding investments toward marketing campaigns that are more effective at generating high-value customers instead of assuming all new customers are of equal value. Marketers cannot wait for the actual customer value to be measured, so understanding how initial behaviors and intelligence can predict the future value will make the ROI measures more accurate. Information such as initial purchase amount, purchase type, demographic profiles, or key questions asked during the sales process can be used in modeling and analysis to serve as future value indicators.

TYPES OF MEASUREMENT PROCESSES

Several techniques are used to measure marketing efforts and analyze data to develop more accurate ROI projections to compare and select the best marketing investment opportunities. Each technique has its advantages and limitations. Applying certain techniques will vary based on the industry, nature of the business model, and customer data access.

Measurements for ROI projections will be necessary to predict the return's gross margin component since the investment will be known or estimated reasonably. Gross margin is driven by incremental customer value, so the measurement analysis typically must focus on capturing customer behaviors and predicting future behaviors.

The following techniques can be used to capture the customer value data points that feed into ROI projections.

- Direct measurement
- Controlled testing Test vs. control Pre/post analysis Experimental design
- Benchmarking assumptions Data mining and modeling Performance indicators as profit drivers Market research
- Assumed impact

BREAK-EVEN ANALYSIS

Their relative values will depend on the shape of the response function and where on that function, the return is evaluated. In other words, the critical difference among the three is the comparison or reference spending level. Because marketing impact on revenue is nonlinear, it matters a great deal in which reference point is chosen.

In summary, we believe there are three critical dimensions of MROI estimates: valuation method, scope/granularity of marketing mix elements assessed, and range of spending evaluated. All three dimensions need to be reported for full transparency and consideration of the concept MROI represents in a particular application.

All methodologies attempt to attribute ROI from the additional financial value to the firm created by marketing spending.

Their differences lie in how the valuation is assessed and the scope and range of marketing efforts evaluated. This scope can range from a specific tactic to a single campaign or even the full marketing mix. As shown in Figure 1, given a scope of marketing, the range of spending evaluated can encompass the entire budget (total), some portion of that budget that makes sense to evaluate as an increment, or the marginal returns of the last dollar spent.

MROI estimates will be more transparently described if those providing the estimates would use the following form: Our analysis measured a (total, incremental, or marginal)9 MROI of (scope of spending) using (valuation method) over time period. For example: 'We measured the total MROI of 2014 trade promotions using baseline-lift to be 34 percent for the Q1, 2014 reporting period.' Baseline-lift refers to the increase in sales above what would have occurred had the trade promotion not been run.

ILLUSTRATIVE MROI SCENARIOS

This section will illustrate each of the MROI return valuation types discussed above and conclude these examples with a statement that would report the valuation method, scope and range of the MROI reported. The examples will start with baseline-lift MROI as the most common and straightforward measure.

Baseline-lift MROI scenario

A technology company selling a software package to small and medium-sized businesses evaluates its targeted marketing campaign. It determines that the campaign generated an incremental 190 units of sales compared to a control group that did not receive the marketing. The integrated campaign consisted of direct mail, e-mail, a landing page with a white paper and an outbound sales contact. The total costs were US $80,000. The company generates a net profit per sale of US $522, for a total of US$99,180 of incremental profit from the 190 units of new sales in the year. The integrated campaign generated a total ROI of 24 percent.

This same method can be applied to a broad range of marketing, from individual tactics to annual multichannel marketing spend when the incremental sales and profits generated from the specific marketing initiative can be determined. The following example is roughly based on a published case study and demonstrates how this method is adapted for different marketing firms.

CHAPTER 10

THE IMPLEMENTATION PROCESS

Increasing your awareness and understanding of marketing ROI and the new concepts presented here has little value on its own. The only way to generate a positive return on the time you've invested is to take actions that will achieve results. No marketing measurement and profit management process is perfect, so there is certainly room for improvement. The question is where to start. Is the right profit focus in place. Are existing measurements consistent across the organization? What barriers must be addressed? How can simple tools, techniques, and training be used to gain momentum.

If the vision is to build an organization-wide or company-wide marketing ROI to take profit optimization to its fullest extent, the process should begin with careful planning. As with any large-scale, enterprise-wide implementation, the best approach is to implement and achieve success incrementally. The marketing ROI process requires change at the campaign, division, and executive level. It will take time to establish standard procedures, refine the accuracy, and shift the existing culture. It's clear from interviews with leading marketing gurus that transition in managing marketing investments will meet some resistance from marketers. The cultural barriers should be taken seriously smooth the transition.

The key steps for implementing ROI measures within the marketing organization are as follows:

Form the cross-functional project team. Many people cringe at the thought of another project that requires a cross-functional team, but it is the right path toward success. Many of the problems and failures with CRM implementations can be linked back to a lack of communication and commitment between organizations in a company.

Review existing marketing measures at the campaign level. The review process needs to address several key questions. How are the current measures aligned with maximizing profits? What is required to introduce ROI as the new primary measure for guiding investment decisions? If ROI measures are in place, are all of the key principles applied to guide accuracy decisions? Are decisions based on the combination of independent, incremental, and aggregated measures?

Establish a commitment and equip the team. Senior management must make a clear statement that aligning marketing decisions with company goals can be greatly improved through the use of ROI measurements. The commitment must be backed by equipping the marketing staff with training and tools. Make the measurement and projection process simple so marketers can apply their expertise in developing strategies and delivering results.

Assess the quality and accessibility of key data. Quality measures depend on timely access to quality data. The Data Warehousing Institute conducted a study that indicated poor data quality is costing businesses more than $600 billion annually. Data integrity issues primarily result from conflicting data in multiple databases or data decay, where good data eventually becomes outdated. Customer value estimates will require quality historical data, accurate results reporting, and reliable modeling of expected future value.

Map out the full-scale marketing ROI process and set standards. The process for using ROI to guide campaign, customer, and corporate profitability will need to be customized to the business model and specific needs of each organization. Having a clear vision for how the company can best apply ROI measurements in the long term will help define how the implementation is phased in. The entire project team needs to have input and buy-in at this stage. The initial standardization of the ROI formula will need to consider the broad range of investments made and measurement issues in different areas to establish a single consistent formula.

Set up a pilot program. The principles of marketing ROI can, for the most part, be initially applied to a subgroup of the marketing organization. Applying ROI tools in strategic development and campaign measurements, prioritizing marketing investments, and maximizing profitability can all work effectively for a small marketing organization. The company can understand the potential benefits and refine the process before implementing it on a large scale. The pilot program should be completed with a highly capable and motivated group to take on a new initiative, manage highly measurable marketing activities, and ideally has some level of control over communications with a customer segment. This last point allows for some initial testing and development of Customer Pathing strategies.

Monitor and adjust the process. Translating principles of ROI measurements into processes that guide better investment decisions will require ongoing assessment and adjustments. Success in the pilot project and each incremental phase should be confirmed by the entire team to identify potential problem areas. Don't fall into the trap of accepting a process that delivers "good news" and rejecting the process if the outcome shows "bad news." Please focus on the quality of the process itself to ensure the output is accurate.

Build an executive control panel. Once the process is considered reliable, the executive control panel can be created. The use of this control panel should go through a testing period as well. Adjustments may be necessary to both the control panel and the core process.

Rollout the ROI processes in phases. While implementing the marketing ROI process, organization-wide should generate additional profits for the company, and it should not be rushed. Each new marketing function brought under the marketing ROI process will require a unique transition. Training and tools need to be implemented with quality as well.

Build Customer Pathing strategies. Viewing profitability at a customer level will vary for different companies based on their preexisting orientation towards customer management versus product management. Companies with CRM initiatives underway should be able to identify and develop Customer Pathing strategies with greater ease. Other companies may need to experiment over time. Two approaches to Customer Pathing can occur simultaneously. The first is identifying where existing campaigns to the same customers have synergy, and the second is developing and testing new strategies that maximize profitability across multiple campaigns.

Manage the marketing investment portfolio. Managing the

budget process as an investment portfolio will follow the successful implementation of the organization's core marketing ROI processes. This function can happen at the division level just as easily as at the corporate level.

Validate projections and adjust assumptions. Decisions will be made based on projected values that must constantly be validated to ensure the projection process is accurate. Benchmark values that are used in place of actual measures must also be kept fresh.

Constantly improve the process. The ROI process requires using data that is available, assumptions, and projections of the future. It is expected to improve the decision-making process but is not expected to achieve 100 percent accuracy. Once the process is up and running, you will have plenty of opportunities to refine and improve the process. Profits and expenses can be brought closer and closer to an individual customer level. Expenses and cost of goods can increasingly be viewed on an incremental basis to identify greater profit opportunities that result as total volume increases, as additional sales are made to current customers. The cost of servicing custom-ers decreases over time.

The process will always have room for improvement. Besides, marketing practices are dynamic and will require changes to keep current with innovations.

THE CROSS-FUNCTIONAL TEAM

Building on the team outlined for the implementation of ROI measurements in his book Measuring Brand Communications ROI, the following roles and responsibilities are outlined:

- Marketing strategy and communications will ensure the ROI measurements can effectively guide investment decisions toward the greatest profits. This group will implement the tools and techniques to maximize the value of more advanced strategic development and analysis processes.

- Sales will provide the connection between actual results and marketing activity, capture intelligence, and serve as the reality check on predictive model analysis.

- Product management will monitor customer needs by value segment, provide pricing-related input, and provide insight into where marketing initiatives can support profit improvements.

- Finance will manage the development and standardization of the ROI formula and process to align with corporate profit goals, set the ROI threshold, and monitor external market conditions

- .Accounting will monitor the process of capturing and applying financial data.

- Research will work to support the measurement process dependent on primary research, establish benchmark measurements where necessary, and collect research data that serve as predictors of future value. Tracking marketing metrics on customer loyalty and understanding customer behavior will continue to be critical to the strategic planning process.

- Information technology will automate the ROI process, provide access to data, ensure data integrity, and facilitate timely reporting of results.

- Business analytics will handle predictive modeling requirements and more advanced results analysis.

- Channel management, including customer service and the website interface, will support the flow of results and provide reps with ROI data that empowers customer-oriented decisions and implements Customer Pathing strategies to make offers and collect intelligence.

- Operations and logistics will provide direction on where profit improvements can be supported through marketing initiatives, and stay current in marketing priorities.

- Human resources will align compensation and performance reviews to new success measures, which must contribute to corporate profit over individual campaign profits.

- Senior executives will need to establish the ROI process as the marketing organization will operate and use the control panel approach to guide the corporation toward improved profitability.

- The initial planning team will need to define the desired benefits, map out the process, and identify potential barriers to success. The team must be made up of individuals committed to the project's success because failure in any department can easily result in a breakdown of the entire process.

FIRST STEPS TO GREATER PROFITS

You've invested your time to go through this book and advance your knowledge in marketing ROI. As with most marketing investments, the big returns take more effort and more time. The list below gives you short-term opportunities to generate additional profits from your current marketing investments.

- **Shift to ROI measures for your next set of campaigns.** If you are not using ROI to prioritize future investments, and gain access to the data, compare the decisions using an ROI analysis. Run the ROI analysis concurrent with your previous measurement process. In many cases, it will lead to the same decision, but finding the difference in a select set of decisions is your first chance to deliver incremental profits.

- **Make any necessary corrections to existing ROI measures**. Review the list of common errors and checkpoints against the key principles outlined throughout this book. The improvement in investment decisions that the result from these corrections can have immediate value.

- **Measure incrementally.** Treat each incremental investment as a decision that must generate an acceptable return. Averaging results using a total ROI value without viewing incremental value can easily lead to costly decisions.

- **Automate basic ROI tools.** Calculate investment limits and create allowable marketing charts to use in strategic planning. Suppose you have not done a similar process in the past. In that case, this can open your mind to innovative strategies based on the combinations of investment levels and sales conversion rates that are possible.

- **Assess data quality for customer value.** Suppose poor quality data is being used to calculate incremental customer value, especially for future value projections. In that case, this could be a hidden drain on profits, turning good measurement practices into a source for bad decisions.

- **Develop select benchmark measures.** What information can make a difference in your ROI calculations but is either too difficult or too expensive to research? This could include the incremental value of a marketing channel or capturing the typical ratio of tracked sales to untracked sales. If this information can lead to better decisions over a long period or across multiple organizations, the investment to measure and establish a benchmark value may be worthwhile.

CHAPTER 11

MARKETING EFFECTIVENESS: IT'S MORE THAN JUST ROI

The task of tying marketing investment to business performance is a serious business, but too often, it is reduced to buzzwords. Terms like ROI, customer value, and optimization all have meaning and relevance but are often used imprecisely to promote very specific solutions to broad business issues. De-cades ago, when few were paying attention to the need to connect marketing to finance, it may have been excusable to use such semantic hooks to grab attention. However, that there is an accepted mandate to understand and measure the financial impact of marketing, it's time to take a more disciplined approach.

ROI VERSUS MARKETING EFFECTIVENESS

The concept of ROI is straightforward. An ROI analysis determines whether various investments achieve satisfactory returns relative to other uses of cash. To wit: Is campaign A, a product-based advertising campaign, better use of cash than campaign B, a brand-building campaign? And does either campaign earn more money for the company than could be made by investments in physical plant and equipment or simply accepting the market rate of return for cash investments?

Whether expressed as a percentage (i.e., return/investment) or as the net present value (NPV) of a stream of cash flows over time, ROI analysis is an important component of the overall process of linking marketing to finance. But it isn't a substitute for understanding how marketing works to achieve business objectives.

Improving marketing effectiveness requires clarifying the strategic intent of all the marketing investments an organization makes, aligning the organization to deliver, and measuring the degree to which those objectives are met. By their nature, many of these business issues don't fit neatly into the ROI framework, but the process of examining them still calls out for as much rigor as possible.

This isn't merely a semantic issue. Understanding the difference between measuring ROI and optimizing marketing effectiveness is as important as distinguishing between a tool and a tool kit, a process and an outcome, an analytical technique and a business solution. Critical decisions such as what to offer, who to target, and how to address the target audience need to be grounded in an overall business strategy. Achieving the desired ROI for a particular activity will be a hollow victory if the overall marketing goals are not met.

The Limits of ROI The limitations of ROI are easy enough to understand when one considers that, by definition, an ROI analysis calls for a well-defined "I" (the investment) and a well-defined "R" (the return).But even when "R" and "I" can't be pinned down precisely, there are still crucial decisions to be made, decisions that carry major financial implications. For example, key strategic directions must be chosen even without precise information on the available investment. Many phases of strategic decision making are fraught with uncertainties, unknowns, and approximations.

Take segmentation. Most organizations use segmentation to identify the most attractive customers, upon whom they will focus on disproportionate resources. The 80/20 rule for customer value often governs; i.e., a small portion of customers account for a huge portion of overall financial value. Thus, segmentation decisions are extremely important, at least somewhat quantifiable, and should be financially driven. But measures of current use, purchase, revenue, and profit, useful though they may be, cannot precisely predict the lifetime value.

But even if NPV cannot be predicted, effective and financially oriented market segmentation can be assembled by combining behavioral data with share-of-wallet surveys and market-responsiveness tracking. This approach, though far from true ROI evaluation, can point up enormous financial implications. The design of products also calls for major financial decisions in the early stages of development. These can defy ROI calculations for several reasons. One is that until the new product platform is finalized, the manufacturing cost can only be approximated. Another is that these manufacturing costs will vary depending on the product's specific features, which aren't fully known until later on in the process.

Between "R" and "I"

Even when "R" and "I" can be precisely stated, focusing too intently on dollars in versus dollars out may not do justice to everything that happens in between. Consider fundamental marketing tasks like creating brand awareness and presence in the market, achieving a place in the customer's consideration set, and positioning the brand with specific benefits relative to the competition. All of these require significant investment before the dollars of return can start pouring in. Several marketing processes have to unfold, on various timeframes, for these intermediate outcomes to lead to customer choice, revenue, and profit.

Some would argue that, because it has no direct financial outcome, an intermediate step such as awareness generation is worthless for assessing business performance. But we believe it's critical to understand these intervening processes. Large budgets might be spent against the wrong customer target, the wrong objective, or the wrong touchpoint. An ROI analysis that focuses only on the result would report a financial failure, but would not shed light on why it happened.

Without an understanding of the flow of the process, it may be difficult to discern why success or failure occurred and what action to take in the case of failure.

Measurement of the intermediate processes will shed light on what is working and what isn't in creating revenue and profit, and what marketing levers should be exercised to achieve the desired outcomes. Creat-ing a diagram to show the influence of the various levers on customer behavior is often useful in identifying where the yield from marketing investment is good and where it falls and can provide a basis for needed improvements and strategic redirection. In financial services, we often depict a chain of intermediate objectives,

We see that each objective, such as driving traffic to a site or facilitating the opening of accounts, is influenced by some but not all marketing levers. In this way, we can tie business and marketing objectives to relevant performance milestones and ensure that appropriate standards are applied in measuring performance. Just as operations managers shouldn't be penalized for revenue shortfalls, marketing pro-cess owners shouldn't be held to standards they can't influence.

If the marketing campaign is supposed to generate qualified leads, and the sales force is supposed to close them, the campaign is only indirectly responsible for sales revenue. The sales force is directly responsible for revenue, but only if it has qualified leads with which to work.

EFFECTIVENESS DEPENDS ON EXECUTION

Finally, it's important to note that financial results are not realized in spreadsheets and presentations, but in the field where actual interactions with customers happen. Some of the most important steps in marketing effectiveness relate to execution against the chosen strategies and tactics.

For segmentation to be actionable, the people who have opportunities to interact with customers need to know the segments and have clear ideas of treating them based on that knowledge. Companies achieve this by creating rich visual descriptions and profiles of customer types and delivering them to all customer-facing employees. For example, marketing managers often display posters depicting representative customers in their work areas to reinforce the idea that employees should be thinking about addressing those types of customers in everything they do.

If product introductions are to succeed, the product must achieve the quality levels specified in its test market phase, receive the promotional support specified in the forecasting models, and secure the field marketing and channel support needed to get the product in front of consumers.

For marketing-mix planning to be useful, the tactical decision-makers need to know how to apply the learning from the models; i.e., how to tailor plans based on working and what's not working. For example, by using simulation tools to run alternative marketing plan scenarios, they can find the ideal weight, schedule, and copy mix, along with selected pricing and distribution levels, to most efficiently and effectively achieve performance goals for sales and profit.

MATCHING MROI METRICS WITH BUSINESS NEEDS

Each commonly used ROI measure we have identified offers unique insight. However, it is necessary to know the conditions under which each ROI measure should be used and to understand that not all ROI metrics are comparable across the different types of measures. Some observations are: The further we move from estimating incremental sales and profits due to marketing and attempt to forecast long-term future returns, in general, the higher will be the risk associated with those forecasts. However, there may be a different degree of uncertainty associated with assessing the degree of the marketing-wrought change in the relevant metric than placing a value on the change. It would make sense that, with higher degrees of risk, the threshold that needs to be exceeded grows as well.

When estimating returns is not only to evaluate past performance but also to improve marketing productivity, more granular estimates will inform the shifting of funds from less to more productive mix elements. This includes changing the focus from 'total' to 'marginal' effect. The latter may allow scaling back or increasing investment in individual mix elements to improve marginal and total MROI. Knowing the potential effect of MROI measures on marketing decisions can help inform the scope, granularity and type of valuation most appropriate to the situation. Certainty, timing costs and returns. Most executives cannot wait until all the data are available before trying to estimate the MROI.

In the case of certain e-commerce transactions, the timing of marketing outlays and incremental revenues generated can be virtually instantaneous. By contrast, recruiting, training and deploying a sales force may take years, and the resulting impact will, therefore, take longer. In many cases, the outlays of marketing expenditures are separated by a considerable amount of time from the results that the spending generates. Feedback, carryover and issues of momentum play more important roles over longer periods. Depending on the time frame considered, we can expect MROI calculations to vary.

Forecasting the future always involves uncertainty, as do attributions of the present rooted in marketing efforts' historical analyses. The degree of uncertainty typically increases as the time horizon expands. Still, other sources of uncertainty can be market turbulence, technological disruptions, competitive actions or reactions, or any number of other factors that companies list in their annual reports. Applying mathematically, rigorous estimation techniques cannot always produce estimates that have a high degree of certainty.

Disclosing that uncertainty in transparent ways to those who rely on those estimates is as much an obligation as is doing our utmost to estimate marketing's contributions accurately. Estimates of uncertainty will likely remain in the eye of the beholder, but full transparency will inform that estimate. The uncertainty may have two important implications for the management application of MROI.

First, the higher the uncertainty, the higher the required MROI is likely to be, as is the case for all financial investments. Secondly, uncertainty metrics of estimates, such as standard deviations, are needed in assessing the MROI. Full development is beyond this paper's scope, although we will return to this issue when spelling out future work needed.

Metrics that are used for estimating MROI vary in their difficulty to measure as well as to value. Increases on either dimension grow the uncertainty in the resulting MROI estimates.

CHAPTER 12
LINKING CUSTOMER ASSET TO FINANCIAL PERFORMANCE

As more firms adopt a customer asset management approach to their business, it has become increasingly important to understand how customer management efforts are related to the firm's financial performance. Of specific interest to shareholders is the relationship between traditional financial measures and customer-centric measures.

The customer-centric measure that has received the most attention is the customer lifetime value (CLV). In this article, the authors argue that the basic CLV model represents a useful foundation from which to begin to fill the gap between marketing actions and shareholder value.

However, much work remains to be done before appropriate models can be developed that reflect the true value to the firm. Specifically, this article elaborates on how factors such as risk associated with customer behavior dynamics, social and competitive effects, and the product life cycle's effect can be incorporated into the basic CLV model.

In general, marketing assets and customer assets have taken on increased prominence in marketing in recent years. This focus on customer assets has been driven, in part, by the recent crash of the dot.com marketplace.

Although the term asset connotes something of financial value, most of the dot.com start-ups were funded based on customer-centric measures such as eyeballs, number of customers, and click-throughs, which have an indirect and often tenuous relationship to shareholder value. Some have focused on these customer-based metrics as one of the chief culprits behind the crash because they provided an erroneous assessment of its ability to leverage its customer relationships to generate sustainable, positive cash flows. If there is one lesson to be learned from the dot.com crash, firms need more effective ways to understand the linkage between customer assets and shareholder value.

The importance of understanding and assessing the value of customer assets is highlighted by the fact that as much as 80% of the value of a firm is composed of intangible assets.

The purpose of this article is to explore ways of linking customer assets to financial performance more effectively. We center our discussion on the Customer Lifetime Value.

(CLV) the model is widely used to assess customer assets (Berger and Nasr, 1999; Dwyer 1997). Usage of the basic model has led to critical insights into marketing management, such as the importance of retention to firm profitability. However, the basic model is relatively simplistic and fails to suitably account for factors such as the risks associated with customer behavior dynamics, social and competitive effects, and the product life cycle. If the customer asset management approach to marketing is to become more than just a slogan, then research must be conducted into these important topics.

This article's basic premise is that customer asset value is correlated with the firm's financial performance and is reflected in traditional financial metrics used to evaluate the firm. To link the customer asset to financial performance, it is necessary to understand customer lifetime value and its indicators. We start with a discussion on the basic model for measuring the value of the customer asset. We then examine how the model can be extended to reflect the customer's contribution to shareholder value more accurately. Our main objective in this article is not to formally derive mathematical formulas but to show which measures or indicators should be useful for valuing the customer base.

MEASURING THE VALUE OF THE CUSTOMER ASSET: THE BASIC MODEL

Before linking customer assets to financial performance, it is crucial to define what those assets are and how to measure them.

The notion that a firm's relationship with a customer can be viewed as an asset is grounded in both the firm's resource-based view (Barney 1991; Hunt and Morgan 1995) and the relationship-marketing paradigm (Dwyer 1997; Morgan and Hunt 1994). From a financial perspective, customers' metaphor as firm assets is consistent with a capital budgeting model. Managers attempt to value projects using asset pricing models, such as the Capital Asset Pricing Model (CAPM) (Brealy and Myers 2000).

What marketers have proposed is that instead of valuing a "marketing project" involving expenditures for the acquisition and retention of customers, it is more useful to change the analysis unit from the project to the customer. Under a customer asset management (CAM) perspective, customers are viewed as risky assets that may produce the firm's cash flow over time.

The value of the customer asset is the expected risk-adjusted profits they produce over time, including the acquisition, retention, expansion, and deletion costs; forecasting the cash flow from even current customers is nontrivial and subject to potential bias. Similarly, adjusting for the risk associated with consumer behavior dynamics is a substantial issue for current customers. It is even more difficult for valuing potential customers that have yet to be acquired. To facilitate a discussion of these difficult issues, we have differentiated the various ways in which the firm can derive value from current and potential customers. As Figure 1 illustrates, customers can create value for the firm in a variety of ways.

The most obvious is from current customers continuing to buy the same thing from a company (Cell 1). The present value of these cash flows (CLV), which depends heavily on the retention rate, is easy to analyze. In its simplest form, by assuming a constant defection rated discount rate k and a constant net margin (profits–retention costs) of m, the value of the annuity attributable to the customer I reduce to $CLV_i = m1_i / (k_1 + d)$

We can incorporate the value of the up-selling opportunity into the base equation by adding a term for individual I's growth rate; this growth rate can be used to value cross-selling opportunities to an existing customer. To the extent, a constant growth rate g_i is a reasonable assumption in the near term (obviously untenable in the long run) and g_i is less than $(k + d)$, customer value is approximated by $CLV_i = m2_i / (k_2 + d - g_i)$

VALUING CROSS-SELLING OPPORTUNITIES

The valuation of cross-selling opportunities is a function of both the likelihood (i.e., probability) of cross-selling and level of success (sales or profits) of cross-selling to both existing and potential customers. It is important to acknowledge that the firm's customer and product management strategies affect both the likelihood and level of cross-selling. Specifically, what product to offer as a cross-buying opportunity is a part of the product management strategy. How to tailor the offering to each customer is a part of the customer management process. Merging these two strategies in a way that optimizes the expected value of the cross-selling opportunity is not a trivial process.

Naturally, prediction and valuation tasks are far more complicated, although not impossible, for potential than existing customers. The level or magnitude of cross-selling success is a key determinant in customer valuation. However, because the valuation computation is based on anticipated future activities, it is also important to address the cross-selling probability.

The likelihood of successful cross-selling (i.e., the cross-selling rate or probability) is an important issue because it reflects the "potential" value of a customer instead of only the value that is currently known. A conservative definition of a customer's potential value to a firm is the profitability of a customer across all products or services in a certain market of the firm (Grant and Schlesinger 1995; Verhoef and Donkers 2001). One should clarify this definition by noting that future purchase behavior drives the magnitude of a customer's potential value. For example, undergraduate students have a low current value in the financial service market. However, to the extent that they are likely to have a well-paid job in the future, they probably have a high potential value.

Accounting for future customer dynamics, particularly those that represent changes in margin contribution or changes in the degree of a customer's loyalty, is critical to linking customer assets to shareholder value. In essence, cross-selling's potential represents the opportunity for growth in cash flows and, equally important, the sustainability of that growth. From a share holder's perspective, firm growth and sustainability of that growth are key to the value of their investment. Addressing the issues of sustainability and growth of customer assets.

This is a summary statement that reflects current and expected future changes in the firm's customer assets. Forecasts of the customer asset's expected future value are achieved by focusing on changes in margins and retention rates of newly acquired customers and existing customers. The flow statement also accounts for lost customer value from defected customers. From a shareholder's perspective, this type of summary is useful because it helps him or her quantifies and monitors one aspect of its intangible assets.

The value of the customer equity flow statement is highly dependent on accurate forecasts. Thus, applying the appropriate forecasting models is essential. With an increasing interest in customer relationship management, direct marketing, and data mining, models that predict response to a direct mailing (Bult and Wansbeek 1995) are estimated based on purchase histories. This information can be aggregated across time and customers to estimate the future value of market segments. The choice of model form depends on the purpose. In the context of predicting customer behavior and implementing one-to-one marketing and cross-selling strategies, managers typically use recency, frequency, and monetary value (RFM) information.

BRAND EXTENSION OPPORTUNITIES

Although the vast literature on brand extensions demonstrates their success in terms of reduced costs and time and higher success rates in introducing new products, there are important limitations. For example, there is concern that a high degree of consistency between the currently offered branded products and the extensions is needed to avoid dilution.

Furthermore, in professional services industries with low consistency between offered services, one might expect few spillover effects of brand associations and satisfaction of the currently consumed services to the new services. From a financial analysis perspective, the valuation of brand extension opportunities is fraught with uncertainty. This uncertainty can be better managed if one understands the relationship between the brand and the customer franchise. One could argue that the value of the brand and its ability to be extended depends in part on the quality of the customer franchise, where quality is reflected in both the current and potential value of that franchise. In terms of our model as described in equations, this means

that brand extensions in markets with customers who have high potential value will have larger values of g_i than markets where the customer's potential future value is lower.

When valuing brand extensions, it is critical to assess how the magnitude of the customer valuation model's growth factor differs across individuals. From a sociological perspective, one could assert that customers (people) exist as part of a complex social system involving other customers, potential customers, and competitors. Within this system, influence is overtly or inadvertently exerted by all members and to all members.

This suggests that the value of the customer asset should be determined, in part, by the nature of the individual's position and influence in the social system and that these social connections should be reflected in the customer valuation model. Some business models rely heavily on the role and interaction between influencers and buyers. For example, in the health care industry, specialists who are likely to be influencers on other specialists or general practitioners are targeted and courted to gain their support for a product.

The specialist is then used as a marketing tool by the firm to garnish support from other potential buyers. Thus, the influencer's realized and potential value is far greater than the direct cash flows that it generates. This can be seen when one considers that some influencers in the health care industry are administrators or other health care workers (e.g., pharmacists and nurses) who do not directly generate any cash flows to the firm. In terms of the CLV model, this means that the magnitude of gi for an influencer has a latent component representing the customer's referral and endorsement value. Thus, an influencer's growth potential is greater than just the margins generated from a greater depth and breadth of buying.

Moving From CLV to Customer Equity

Up to this point, we have discussed the basic CLV model, which is an individual-level model. Another basic measure that is often referenced when discussing a firm's financial performance is customer equity (CE). The CLV model and the CE model are directly related. CE is just the aggregation of the expected lifetime values of a firm's firm's existing customers and the expected future value of newly acquired customers. As shown in equation 4, CE is the sum of equations 2 and 3 for all existing and new customers.

A basic premise of customer asset management is that firms should seek to optimize their CE. Unfortunately, in a resource-constrained environment, optimizing CE involves balancing trade-offs between existing customers' investments and investments in new customers.

These trade-offs are reflected in the magnitude of the margin and expenditure terms of equations 2 and 3. Specifically, in the model for existing customers (Model 2), the margin is highly dependent on retention costs. In the new customer model, the margin from purchases and the acquisition investment significantly influences customer value. Because all firms lose customers for one reason or another, it is critical that they carefully manage the balance between acquisition and relationship maintenance investments. Investments made in the customer's influence both their current and future behavior.

The impact of investments on future behavior makes CE management challenging and necessarily a dynamic process, particularly as the composition of the firm's cufirm's database evolves. While CE is the aggregate measure that reflects the overall or total value of a firm's cufirm's assets, when developing customer management strategies and tactics, it helps discuss the value of individual customers and the factors that influence that value. Thus, the remainder of our discussion focuses on the individual-level model.

EXTENDING THE BASIC CLV MODEL

Customer asset valuation models are still in their infancy. Thus, it is not surprising that the basic model contains numerous deficiencies that limit its effective application to a wide variety of markets. In this section, we attempt to identify some of these deficiencies and, where possible, to explore possible solutions. An unresolved challenge for marketers is how to adjust for the differential risk of various customers. Surely, money invested in a long time customer with a steady purchase history is less at risk than money invested in a prospect with little knowledge about the firm. The customer profitability model discussed in the previous section, which is widely used by businesses in a variety of markets, assumes that all customers are equally risky and discounts their revenue streams at the same discount rate.

As illustrates and as was suggested by the prior discussion, the level of uncertainty about the outcomes of a firm's mafirm 'sg efforts increases as the firm focuses its efforts on new customers and new product categories. By relying on a single discount rate (usually the weighted average cost of capital), the firm is undervaluing its longtime customers and overvaluing its prospects.

This is not a serious concern as long as the customer profitability model is used as a general strategic tool to guide retention efforts and the like. However, an increasing number of firms are using these profitability models to allocate scarce marketing dollars. The current model could induce them to underspend on current customers and overspend on acquisition efforts.

The basic model is problematic in its treatment of risk in another regard. As we have previously noted, the basic CLV model is a derivative of the CAPMthat adjusts for risk through the risk-adjusted return (RAR) in the denominator. But what are the sources of risk that might affect the value of a customer asset? Cash flows derived from a customer are at risk due to various factors such as defection, reduced wallet share, reduced size of a wallet, and increased cost to serve.

The risk factor that has been of greatest concern to marketers has been defection. Indeed, the probability of defection is explicitly included in the model by adjusting the retention rate's expected cash flows. These risk-adjusted cash flows should be discounted at a lower discount rate, yet this is not typically done. As a result, the basic model may systematically discount expected cash flows and undervalue the customer asset.

CAPTURING SOCIAL EFFECTS

Implicit in the basic customer valuation model is the notion that a customer' station to the firm can be valued in isolation. Those values can then be summed to form an estimate of the firm's firm' Ostberg and Deighton 1996). Although valuing a tangible asset such as a machine in isolation may be appropriate, the assumption is more problematic when applied to customers. Customers exist as part of a complex social network, including other customers, potential customers, and customers of competitors' way. These customers can have a substantial impact on their contribution to the firm's performance' silly. Word-of-mouth (WOM) communications have long been recognized as an important factor influencing consumer' products (). Indeed, marketers generally acknowledge that.

Customers who spread positive WOMare worth more than those who do not or who spread negative WOM. However, the basic model fails to account for social interactions such as WOMto firm profitability. As a result, it can lead to substantial errors in estimating customer profitability.

There are several avenues by which social processes such as Women contribute to the customer asset's value. Previously, we mentioned how social effects could affect brand or product adoption and influence the growth factor. Another means is through reducing the acquisition costs of the firm. When a firm acquires a satisfied customer who spreads positive WOM, it also acquires any customers the customer might convince purchase in the future. The value of these additional acquisitions can be substantial. For example, a recent study involving hairstyling customers found that, on average, the spread between 2.85 and 3.88 WOMincidents after each hairstyling appointment, depending on the type of establishment. When the value of this WOM-was incorporated into a CLV model, the value of WOM ranged from 97% of the base value of a customer to 214%, depending on the type of salon (Hogan, Lemon, and Libai 2001a). Thus, the value of a customer asset can increase substantially when the customer is valued in the context of the social system in which he or she resides.

Marketers miss a substantial amount of a customer's value by treating the customer as an isolated entity. In addition, to decreasing acquisition costs, social processes among customers may help increase retention rates as current customers share their experiences, as in so-called brand communities. Thus, the return derived from a firm's in-firm 'sets in service quality may be substantially higher than predicted by established methods such as the return on equity (ROQ)

DEVELOPING A TRULY INDIVIDUAL CUSTOMER PROFITABILITY MODEL

Few advances in marketing during the past several years have been heralded more than the advent of CRM, which promises to enable firms to adapt strategy decisions to the individual level by leveraging the vast amount of customer information gathered through a dizzying array of touchpoints. However, there is a reason to question whether the promise of value-based individual marketing can be fulfilled using extant models. Perhaps one of the most critical shortcomings of the basic model is that it assesses only the value of an "average "customer" by using" customer cohorts to forecast future sales and estimate retention rates. The distinction between an average and individual model is important because, thanks to interactive technologies, the firm possesses substantial information about individual customers, purchase behavior, and shopping habits.

Yet, how can this information be incorporated into a customer profitability model that only has inputs for "average" "custome" s? Clearly, there is a need for a valuation mocustomerted for individual customers (probably using Bayesian methods) that can be updated as the firm learns more about its habits and lifestyle. A concept in CRM that attempts to make a summary or average measurements more useful and representative of the entire databases is the idea of duration-adjusted measures

The basic premise behind a duration adjusted measure is that customers behave differently at different customer life stages. For example, a newly acquired customer who is still in the trial and learning stages of his relationship with the firm may be more likely to defect than an existing or core customer who has had extensive experience with the firm. Another factor that supports the use of duration-adjusted measures is that it is not uncommon that a firm's cufirm's database will have a disproportionate number of existing customers versus newer customers.

Moreover, new to existing customers will change as the affirm and retention strategy changes. A typical summary measure (i.e., a non-duration-adjusted measure) simply averages the value of a single measure (e.g., retention rate) over several periods. This average becomes the average metric typifying behavior for the entire database of customers.

In contrast, when computing duration-adjusted summary statistics, firms acknowledge that newly acquired customers may have dramatically different "averages" than co "e customers and that the customer portfolio does not have equal numbers of each customer type. Thus, a duration-adjusted weighted average will be more reflective of the dynamics in the firm's acfirm and retention strategies. However, more complex than applying duration adjustments to measures affirmed is also a rich literature in finance on stochastic valuation models that could provide a foundation for future research. These models have been applied to various assets ranging from machinery to large-scale projects and could potentially be adapted to customer assets. The models assume a stochastic process for how an asset's value evolves over time and then updates the value of the particular asset based on information gained through experience with the particular asset.

Marketers could develop stochastic models for various customer segments and, upon acquisition, value the customer according to the information known at the time. As the firm learned more about the customer, his value to the firm would be updated in two ways. First, the customer' should be adjusted based on the actual purchase.

Behavior. Thus, if a customer purchased more than expected, the value could be adjusted based on the underlying stochastic process. Second, if the firm learns that the customer had been placed in the wrong stochastic process upon acquisition, it can switch the customer to a more appropriate process. For example, suppose the firm acquires a customer, I believe, to be a single woman between the ages of 18 and 34 and assesses her value based on a stochastic model describing similar customers. However, when the firm learns through an online survey that the customer is married with two children, it can switch the valuation model to one that reflects that segment's purchases. Thus, using this approach, the firm can incorporate both purchase and demographic information to assess its customer's value.

ACCOUNTING FOR MANAGERIAL FLEXIBILITY

Another limitation of the basic CLV model is that it implicitly assumes that the firm adopts a fixed strategy for managing the customer asset. This assumption stems from using a net present value (NPV)-based approach to valuation that requires the firm to forecast future revenues, costs, and investments and discount them based on the cost of capital and the specific risk of the investment. Critics of the NPV approach contend that it provides an inaccurate estimate of value in many circumstances because of its underlying assumption that future investments' timing and magnitude are fixed at the time of valuation.

Although this assumption might be suitable for certain investments in capital equipment where the investment occurs at the time of purchase, it may not be appropriate for customer assets. The firm makes ongoing investments in retention and cross-selling depending on customer information gained during the relationship life. When investments in an asset are staged over time, managers have an opportunity to learn from previous investment outcomes and use that knowledge to make more effective decisions going forward. This ability to learn from experience before making investments can be quite valuable to the firm, yet the value of that learning is not captured in the traditional CLV metric. Consequently, the basic CLV metric can substantially undervalue customer assets because it does not recognize that managers have flexibility in determining the timing and magnitude of future investments in retention, cross-selling, and even abandonment.

These potential future investments have similar characteristics to financial options in which the firm has the right, but not the obligation, to invest in the asset. Incorporating managerial flexibility to either invest in or divest an asset is the central theme of the emerging literature on real options. The real-options analysis captures the value of the flexibility that firms have when making relationship-related investments.

BEYOND CLV: EXPLORING THE DIRECT LINK BETWEEN CUSTOMER ASSETS AND FINANCIAL PERFORMANCE

For publicly traded companies, the ultimate goal is to explain and manipulate market capitalization or shareholder value.
Linking marketing actions through customer value to changes in market metrics (e.g., market value-added, or MVA) represents one way to achieve this goal. In doing so, an important distinction exists between change/flow measures and state measures. Whereas measures such as economic value added (EVA) and MVA focus on changes in financial performance, others such as market capitalization measure performance level. Still, other metrics such as ROX (RO = return on; X might be advertising or investment or assets or sales) provide diagnostics that are useful in assessing the impact of managerial actions and a "snapshot" view of "performance.

. The reverse arrows suggest that there is value in working backward in linking metrics that financial markets track (such as price/earnings (P/E) and market-to-book (M/B) ratios to customer value and then to marketing actions that create customer value (product development, advertising, etc.). Measures of stock market performance (last column, Figure 2) that might be linked to measures of customer value include the following:

Market capitalization. Market capitalization has been linked to intellectual property value, such as marketing experts and customers.
• Difference between market capitalization and book value. Market capitalization is the market value of all outstanding shares of a firm. Book value is the difference between a firm's as firm 'snd liabilities.
The difference between market and book value is assumed to be due to intangible and hard-to-measure assets such as brand equity, intellectual property, process knowledge, and human capital. The magnitude of this difference is driven in part by a firm CE. The growth and dynamics in this difference should mirror the dynamics in CE.

• Market-to-book (M/B) ratio. This is the ratio of market capitalization to the book (or accounting value) of a firm. The relationship between brand value and M/B is demonstrated. Using this linkage to brands, one could extend it to customers and customer potential value.

A q value greater than 1 indicates that the firm has intangible assets. These assets enable a firm to create earnings over its tangible assets and achieve an abnormal return on invested capital relative to its competitors. The linkage to customer assets is that the larger the CE, the larger the q value. An interesting analysis would be to compute the firm' CE.-firm'the CE total to the value for the firm's tafirm's assets' replacement costs. Then compute the q value using the customer equity added into the denominator of the ratio. If the firm's vafirm's n is highly dependent on its customer assets, the revised ratio should move closer to 1.

• EVA and MVA. According to some, EVA is the financial performance measure that comes closer than any other measure to capture an enterprise's true economic profit. Simply put, EVA is the net operating profit minus the cost of capital employed to produce those profits for that year. EVA is frequently used, but the empirical link between increasing EVA due to investments in marketing assets has to be proven. EVA has been very popular in corporate financial management and is available through Stern Stewart, a leading proponent of EVA analysis.

The critical linkage to explore is the percentage of EVA created by customer assets. For example, it might be possible to show that superior customer value leads to higher margins either due to higher prices (from end consumers) or lower distribution costs (due to clout over distributors or "customer").. MVA" tracks the change in mark cap. The utility of demonstrating the impact of EVA and MVA through customer value provides a direct link between marketing strategy and changes in a firm's firm's fortunes.

• Margins, Earnings, and Cash Flow. The stock market pays a great deal of attention to firms' ability to maintain or increase margins. Lowering of prices and, therefore, margins are often viewed as evidence of vulnerability to competitive inroads. For example, a reduction in Marlboro prices by Philip Morris in the early 1990s was interpreted as the "death of "brand equity" and had "a ripple effect on stocks' price across the consumer packaged goods industry. Earnings depend both on market share and net margins. However, the market often focuses more on margins because market share metrics tend to be more stable quarter to quarter. Because of accounting vagaries, earnings can often be manipulated. This has led to a focus on cash flow (earnings adjusted for interest, depreciation, and investments).

• P/E and price/cash flow (P/CF) ratios. Generally, firms with higher growth prospects and lower risk (volatility and vulnerability of cash flows). Marketing and customer management have an obvious impact on these factors. Brand loyalty (or customer retention) is especially important in determining financial value. Unfortunately, marketers tend to focus more on revenue and market share and less on the long-term impact of retention in demonstrating the value they create.

• ROX and CFROI (cash flow returns on investments). These are important diagnostic metrics and are often used to compare projects and track success temporally. Once again, the role of marketing actions and customer value, although implicit (e.g., that customer satisfaction ultimately leads to greater returns or profits), needs to be made explicit by showing the direct impact on share and margins

In linking customer value to financial performance (or back to its marketing activity antecedents), the first stage is to establish correlations (i.e., related). For example, Lane and Jacobson (1995) showed that brand extension announcements lead to abnormal returns on stocks (i.e., returns over those predicted by changes in the market index), thus establishing a link between marketing activity and stock price. Brand equity is related to a lower cost of capital and, therefore, higher market capitalization.

However, the ultimate goal is to demonstrate how changes in customer and brand value lead to changes in financial market value. One example that demonstrated this relationship using a customer profitability model is the work of Gupta that compared the value of the customer base to the market capitalization for several Internet firms, have shown that site characteristics measured by Nielsen/Netratings, such as stickiness, reach, and loyalty was correlated with share prices both in 1999 and 2000 reported positive associations between satisfaction and firm profitability as return on investment. Interbrand demonstrates a strong correlation between brand reputation and financial performance.

But the alternative explanation of reverse causation has yet to be ruled out. Finally, Kim showed a strong relationship between the net present value of cash flows attributable to customers and stock prices in the cellular telephone industry. If replicated in other industries, such findings will demonstrate that shareholder value is indeed linked inextricably to customer value. Consequently, research on new measurement models linking stocks (customer assets) and flows (changes in customer assets) to changes in financial performance measures are particularly fruitful. On the positive side, it is worth noting that although other assets depreciate, customers and brands are those only assets that appreciate.

CHAPTER 13
MARKETING ASSET MROI SCENARIO

Two railroads merge, creatinThereThe new firm is not well known, and the stock price falls below what top management believes it should be. A $100MM advertising campaign in the financial press is launched. Relating to the industry, the new firm's firm' sap grows by $115MM after one year attributed to the advertising that they do not believe would have occurred otherwise. Based on their historical P/E ratio and that of the industry, the CFO decides the campaign is a success by comparing the increase in market capitalization for equivalent earnings to the campaign's cost. The MROI is the increase in market cap of $115MM minus the advertising cost divided by the advertising ($115MM − $100MM)/$100MM = 15%. Our analysis identified an incremental 15% MROI of the advertising campaign using the year's marketing assets valuation method.

RESPONSE METRICS AND THEIR CONNECTION TO MROI

Our discussion should be clear that the computation of a baseline sales performance is essential for the estimation of MROI. In straight business terms, any time we wish to assess the ROI of marketing activity, we need to know what would have happened (to sales and any metrics derived from sales) if said marketing activity had not taken place. The answer to this important question leads us to discuss relevant marketing models, i.e., abstract representations of demand for the brand in the presence vs. absence of marketing activity, i.e., the estimation of marketing impact. Indeed, we may find that marketing spending occurs and there is no increase in sales. Yet, to assess this fairly, it would be necessary to assess what would have happen-reflect pending had not taken place. This again requires the use of the marketing mentioned above mix models.

Marketing impact that has financial consequences comes in three forms: either cost savings, unit sales impact, or change in margin impact, or some combination of the three. The most straightforward method for assessing impact is a simple experimental design (A/B testing, where B is the control group). Some markets (e.g., regions, individual customers, or periods) are exposed to marketing activity, and others are not. Such an A/B test reveals two points on the demand curve, as shown in Figure 1(following References). In most applications, the marketing executive will make a linear interpolation between the two and derive the MROI as follows:

MROI = (gross margin (condition A) – gross margin (condition B) –

marketing spend (condition A)) / marketing spend (condition A).

Its limitation offsets the ease of interpretation of such test results: two data points are insufficient to characterize a response function. Obtaining more data points quickly becomes expensive in time and execution costs. Many companies choose to assess their MROI by building so-called marketing mix models or market response models (see Hanssens, Parsons, & Schultz 2001 for an elaboration). Such models should explicitly incorporate marketing phenomena that have important consequences for MROI, including:

Nonlinear response effects, in particular, concave and S-shaped response

INTERACTIONS AMONG THE MARKETING MIX VARIABLES

Sales impact that is distributed over time (so-called carryover effects). Non-zero sales with zero marketing spend. Ideally, although rarely, these models should include competitive spending and competitive reaction to firms' changes.

These considerations could result in complex response models that may fit sales data well but are tedious to interpret for marketing managers. Fortunately, relatively simple response models, such as the multiplicative (Cobb-Douglas) function from economics, exist that can meet the criteria above and still result in easy-to-interpret measures of marketing lift. The most common of those is the response elasticity e: e(marketing) = % change in sales / %change in marketing spend.

So, for example, e(advertising) = 0.08 means that a ten percent increase in advertising Spend results in a 0.8 percent increase in sales ((10)*(.08)), all else equal. Elasticities can be shown to be estimated directly from a multiplicative model. If an S-shaped response is suspected (which is common but involves more than one elasticity value), a model specification test can be run on the data at hand (see, e.g., Hanssens and Dekimpe (2008) for the specifics).

Response elasticity is a measure of top-line lift due to marketing, which is the basis for MROI calculation. Numerous studies in marketing science have resulted in various empirical generalizations, for example, advertising elasticity averages 0.1 but is much higher for new products relative to an established product, and sales calls have an average elasticity of 0.35

Importantly, marketing elasticity and MROI are not the same, as one is a top-line and the other a bottom-line impact measure. However, they are connected via the well-known Dorfman-Steiner theorem (discussed in Hanssens, Parsons, & Schultz 2001) for optimal marketing spending, where optimal means profit-maximizing. Illustrated here for the simple case of two marketing spending categories, say, TV advertising (TV) and paid search advertising (PS), the Dorfman-Steiner theorem specifies that allocations that follow the simple ratio TV/PS = e(TV)/e(PS) results in maximum profits. At that spending level, the marginal MROI for the two media will be equal to zero. At the margin, spending fewer dollars on TV or PS will result in the brand "leaving "money on the table," and spending more will result in profit loss (despite possible sales gain).

TV = e(TV) * gross margin
PS = e(PS) * gross margin

So, if the gross margin of a brand is 50% and the TV elasticity is 0.08, the optimal TV spend = (.50)*(.08) = 4 percent of sales. At that spending level, the marginal MROI will be zero.

Naturally, response elasticities can be extended to represent long-term impact rather than short term sales impact. This can be achieved in two different ways:

1. Change the performance metric to a metric that is intrinsically long-term oriented, such as brand equity and customer equity. Some of the case studies in this paper will use customer equity as a long-run brand health metric. If reliable external estimates of brand equity are available, then brand-response elasticities may be derived as well.

2. Infer the long-term impact of marketing on sales econometrically. For example, suppose a doubling of advertising lifts sales by 10 percent in the short-run (i.e., elasticity = 0.1). In that case, half of that increase becomes permanent (e.g., due to newly gained customers becoming brand loyal), the long-term response elasticity would be .05. Various time-series methods discussed in Hanssens, Parsons, & Schultz (2001) may be used for this purpose. Naturally, since the time horizon now extends well into the future, it is advisable to discount the future sales lifts to obtain a net present value estimation of marketing impact.

In many cases, MROI is derived from individual business events, as illustrated in the scenarios above. So long as the causal connection between input (marketing) and output (sales and the other components in the sales funnel and the follow-on impact to the firm) is unambiguous, this is fine, at least for evaluating the ROI of historical campaigns. However, when planning future marketing efforts, we need sales projections with and without the marketing investment. That requires either A/B testing (which is a form of test marketing) or formal statistical models of brand demand.

The latter can be used not only for MRI estimation but also for sales forecasting and determining optimal marketing allocations. As we shall see below, profit maximization is quite different from chasing high MROI

BASELINE-LIFT MROI SCENARIO

A technology company selling a software package to small and medium businesses evaluate its targeted marketing campaign and determines that the campaign generated an incremental 190 units of sales compared to a control group that did not receive the marketing.

The integrated campaign consisted of direct mail, e-mail, a landing page with a white paper and an outbound sales contact. The total costs were $80,000. The company generates a net profit per sale of $522 for a total of $99,180 of incremental profit from the 190 units of new sales in the year. The integrated campaign generated a total ROI of 24% (calculated as ($99,180 – $80,000)/$80,000) using the Baseline-Lift MROI

VALUATION METHOD.

This same method can be applied to a broad range of marketing, from individual tactics through annual multi-channel marketing spend when the incremental sales and profits generated from the specific marketing initiative can be determined. The following example is roughly based on a published case study. It demonstrates how this method is adapted for different marketing campaigns, the 'country' coordinated effort to promote the United States to international travelers. The campaign spent $72 million on various media ads in the 2013 fiscal year, targeting tourists from eight different countries. According to a research study, it increased visitors from these countries of 1.1 million (2.3%) over the expected visitor levels in 2013. Those visitors spent about $3.4 billion in the same fiscal year. While many benefits can result from this campaign, from a purely financial standpoint, many tax-funded tourism organizations will run the analysis based on the tax returns generated, with the hope of recovering or exceeding the expenditure made.

If we assume an average corporate tax rate of 12%, the $3.4 billion in incremental revenue will generate $408 million in taxes. The total ROI of the FY2013 Brand USA campaign is estimated to be 466% (calculated as ($408MM –$72MM)/$72MM) based on the Baseline-Lift MROI valuation method for the fiscal year 2013. It should be noted that often MROI can be a rather large number given these estimates tend only to spend and do not reflect the allocation of the fixed costs of infrastructure that often make the delivery feasible. If more plants or staff were necessary to be added to deliver on the increase in sales, then that expenditure would have to be considered. Otherwise, it is the impact of marketing spend utilizing the firm's existing under-utilized capacity fully.

Comparable cost MROI scenario
Most of an internet retailer' retailer' is currently generated through

paid search advertising. The cost per click-through (CTR) for a group of search terms is averaging $1.50, and the firm is spending $6,000 per year on search advertising. Assume the CMO decides to invest $1,000 on improving the site's or site's search ranking, increasing organic clicks migrating away from paid search, thereby reducing paid costs to $4,000 per year. Total traffic (organic and paid search) remains the same.

The reduction in search advertising spending for the year is $2,000 while the overall traffic has remained the same. The MROI is the cost savings in paid search minus the improvement cost to generate the search traffic divided by these costs or ($2000-$1000)/$1000 = 100%.
W estimate the total annual MROI of the site improvements on a comparable cost basis to be 100% for the year. There could be additional benefits in years to come and through subsequent purchases from the acquired customers.

FUNNEL MROI SCENARIO

A company launches a content-based marketing campaign at the cost of $30,000, generating 6,000 views of its educational video. Based on historical funnel tracking of similar campaigns, they project 12% of viewers will become qualified leads within six weeks, and 10% of those leads will convert to a sale in 9 months, resulting in 72 sales. At a profit of $500 per sale, the campaign is projected to generate $36,000 in incremental profit for an estimated short-term ROI of ($36,000-$30,000)/$30,000=20%.

The analysis identified a total MROI for the educational videos of 20% using the funnel conversion method for the nine months. Customer equity MROI scenario. A small financial institution catering to the high wealth segment has 10,000 customers with average annual profits of $2,000 per customer. A senior bank executive was concerned about the attrition rate among its customers, which stood at 20% annually, somewhat higher than the competitive benchmark of 15%. She authorized a $4 million investment in customer service enhancement, including upgrades to the bank's bank' technology and higher customer support staffing.

One year after implementation, the bank's cubank's attrition rate had dropped to 17%, while the sector benchmark stayed the same. There are different ways to calculate customer equity. This bank's bank was to look at the future profit stream of its customer base, ignoring any changes in customer acquisition levels or the time value of money. Before the service improvement, customer equity (CE) stood at (10,000*$2,000)/0.20=$100MM. After the improvement, the CE rose to (10,000*$2,000)/0.17=$117.6 million. The total MROI of the retention initiative using the Customer Equity MROI valuation method is 340% (calculated as (17.6MM − 4MM)/4MM) over the acquired customers' life. The return is considered "equity" "and not" "increment" al profit" as means "red with the Baseline-Lift method because the future profits require additional marketing investments and can easily change over time based on other factors.

CHAPTER 14
MARKETING BY THE NUMBERS: HOW TO OPTIMIZE MARKETING

ROI the Global 1000 spends on marketing and advertising across all media. It's no sIt's amount, but it's apart 'sly not enough to halt the erosion of customer loyalty that's that' celebrating during the past decade. According to CNW Marketing Research, actual customer loyalty (i.e., repeat purchase of the same brand) in the auto industry has dropped 5 percent from 1990 to 2000. It continues to decline than one-third of all brands analyzed dropped in customer loyalty by double-digit percent – some by more than 30 percent.

1 In the North American automobile market alone, this loyalty decline accounted for nearly $25 billion in sales that switched hands
2. To quote an old song, "Somethin," Something' sg here; what it is ain'texacain'texactlyCertain "y, today's today 'ss are a fickle lot. When their demands and needs are not readily met, they won't heswon't to shift brands, find a new distributor, partner with another manufacturer, or seek an alternative service provider. But should the nation be enough to help persuade customers to demonstrate more loyalty to brands and companies?

The real dilemma is how and where the dollars are allocated. Some amount of marketing expenditures are hitting their mark because companies are still in business.
However, few if any companies can determine with any certainty which marketing programs consistently return genuine business benefits to the company, which simply siphon away profits. And that inability to determine the ROI of each marketing activity undermines the entire marketing effort – precisely at a time when companies need a highly effective marketing function the most.

EFFECTIVE MARKETING IS ESSENTIAL

Nothing about today's today 'ss or markets is certain; the fact that marketers know all too well. With change now a constant, marketing managers recognize that they have to develop effective marketing programs to grow to keep existing customers, bring in new ones, open unexplored markets, and create new opportunities in those markets thought to be mature. Well-designed and well-implemented marketing activities, they know, are key to generating sales and revenues.

For many companies that sell fast-moving consumer goods, a major marketing effort – including new-product development, distribution, advertising, and promotion –can generate as much as 40 percent of short-term sales. In the consumer electronics industry, the introduction and promotion of new products can stimulate as much as 80 percent of that sale

Even old products can find new life in rapidly developing markets to support an effective marketing function. For example, introducing new technology into certain markets can send old products into a tailspin – witness the fate of products such as rotary telephones, PDAs, and computer processors.

In addition to capturing value from previously untapped sources, an effective marketing campaign is invaluable in maintaining and increasing customer satisfaction and loyalty.

Marketing is the principal communicator of a company's promise and customer experience – everything the company says it will provide through its products and services, including customer satisfaction, support, technical solutions, guarantees, price points, discounts and coupons, and prompt distribution, and the like. Effective marketers who ensure there's between what the company promises and what it delivers are much more likely to experience strong customer loyalty and repeat business than competitors who frequently let customers down or confuse them with conflicting messages and experiences.

WRONG MARKET, WRONG MESSAGE

To be sure, an effective marketing program is essential to business success today, regardless of industry. However, even the leaders discover that their marketing capabilities let them down just when they need them most. And they're they 'for it at the cash register and on Wall Street. In some companies, their marketing limitations have manifested themselves in missed opportunities. Levi Strauss is a classic example. The purveyor of jeans that were once the epitome of cool and the object of desire by teens and young adults everywhere, Levi Strauss lost its way in the 1990s. Confused by the new wave of customers with different needs and values, the company struggled to develop relevant new products. While selected Levi's jeLevi's campaigns have been memorable, others have been flops, and campaigns are changed regularly.

Ineffective marketing also has resulted in inconsistent customer experiences for thereof many businesses. Several companies suffered setbacks from their ill-conceived plans for Internet shopping. They created sites where customers could make purchases, touting how "easy and "convenient" it was "o shop on the Web. But customers who tried to return items were disappointed. Web-only retailers hadn't threaded through how they'd dethey 'DH returns, and the resulting expense and confusion customers endured eventually drove them away. Many retailers with brick-and-mortar stores fared no better in the early days. They confounded customers who tried to return a Web-purchased item to a store in the mall by refusing to accept such returns. Stung by the experience, many customers took their business elsewhere.

Even a venerable company like Coca-Cola has not been immune to marketing missteps that can inflict considerable damage on its brand, masterfully crafted for decades. Seeking to restore earnings growth two years ago, Coke embarked on a major reorganization that pushed decision-making out of its company headquarters into business units worldwide. The move backfired, however, as the companies HQ marketing team left the company. Left to their own devices, the business units disbanded the global agency network. They created several embarrassing, conflicting, and ineffective ad campaigns, resulting in two years of lower growth in sales volume, a reduced market share, and loss of ground to PepsiCo in the brand space.5 Coke is now reconstructing its global approach.

WHY MARKETING ROI IS IN DECLINE

So what's what 'slim? Why have once-proud companies begun swinging back and forth from global to local or modern to traditional positioning as they struggle to find the right concept, the right message, and the right market for their products? Why are businesses of all types finding it so difficult to keep pace with customers who have become more mobile, sophisticated, demanding, and fickle? Why have so many marketing efforts produced such poor results despite investing significant company resources? Five factors are largely responsible for the current state of affairs:

- Use of obsolete marketing tools
- Fragmented nature of marketing processes
- Lack of objective measurements
- Image of marketing as a creative pursuit that's that' sect to rigor and discipline
- Lack of consistency and broad corporate perspective Obsolete Tools

One of the most significant marketing problems is that marketing professionals in many companies are using outdated practices and tools to plan and execute marketing programs. Marketing today still is largely based on the brand management principles pioneered by Procter & Gamble in the 1920s. These principles have been successful in the past.

A prime example is how ineffectual marketing techniques can become institutionalized. Many mass-marketing techniques, such as broadcast advertising, continue to be very effective while others, such as couponing and excess price promotion, have spiraled out of control. Historically, brand building accounted for more than 50 percent of a budget, yet, in the 1990s, most brand-building investments dropped to between 20 percent and 40 percent of total investments, with the rest going to trade and price promotions.

Numerous studies, including the trade-driven Efficient Consumer Response initiative in the grocery industry, have confirmed the wastefulness of promotional tools such as couponing. And yet their use continues to grow.

REINING IN MARKETING ROI

It's clear' sat the time has come for companies to measure and improve marketing investment return. But how? The first order is to adopt a new approach to marketing that consists of six major steps:

- Quantify the effects of past marketing efforts
- Analyze competitive performance
- Identify underperforming initiatives before they become too costly
- Establish accountability for each marketing element
- Pinpoint products and markets where significant growth is possible
- Reallocate marketing resources to capture those new opportunities

Such an approach would have been impossible to adopt in the past due to the lack of both the necessary technology and the willingness among the marketing community to embrace it. However, better access to data and newer marketing techniques, including econometrics, ROI measurement, and allocation software, make such analyses feasible; and the recent difficulties that many companies have experienced are providing the impetus for senior executives' of marketing performance (and, subsequently, grudging acceptance among marketers that new methods are needed).

QUANTIFY THE EFFECTS OF PAST MARKETING EFFORTS

Marketing executives are finally coming under pressure – from CEOs, CFOs, and shareholders, among others – to quantify the effects of past marketing campaigns. Most companies conduct annual marketing analysis, relating marketing investments to top-line sales and market share. They then make decisions for the next year's years without adequately quantifying the effects of each marketing element's elements n growth and profitability. However, it is much easier to gather all the data and measure that effort in great detail. Most consumer industries have good access to monthly and weekly industry sales data. For example, Supermarket Scan data can provide weekly transactions of fast-moving consumer goods. In contrast, two main national pharma cist-report systems – IMS and Scott Levin – provide similar high-quality pharmaceuticals data. Traffic to Web sites can be measured daily in terms of the number of visitors and their purchase behavior.
Similarly, marketing activities can be recorded with increasing specificity and granularity.

Once the data is collected and organized, marketers can use time-series analysis to determine which elements of the marketing program have delivered results and which elements have underperformed. Then the marketing mix can be reallocated to accelerate growth or cut costs. Given today's today' say, marketing directors have no excuse for not being able to explain the return their
marketing investments have yielded.
Judgment, experience, and creativity will always play a leading role in marketing, but they should not be applied to the exclusion of a

KAMALDEEP SINGH

disciplined approach to ROI.

DEVELOP INSIGHTS INTO COMPETITIVE PERFORMANCE

It is easier for a company to quantify the effects of its marketing efforts but more difficult to estimate those of its competitors. Managers do not have all the resources they would like to evaluate how the competition is performing.

Nevertheless, using the same techniques just described, it is possible to examine competitive performance and assess its effectiveness. Thus, it is possible to track most competitors' and activities in terms of advertising and price promotion, performing the same time-series analysis, and piecing together a fairly detailed and insightful image of key competitocompetitors's and weaknesses.
full marketing-mix analysis should be part and parcel of any company's aspany 'set and a holistic view of the entire industry and all its players. Such an analysis can provide deep insight into the nature of competition and give the company undertaking the review a clear competitive advantage. Not only will company managers learn more about their marketing processes, but they may also come away with a better understanding of the competition than competitors have of themselves.

IDENTIFY UNDERPERFORMING INITIATIVES

Time-series analysis reveals important insights into how different parts of the marketing mix are performing. It can track, for example, the base sales of a product or a brand as an indicator of how loyal customers are, regardless of special promotions or marketing blitzes.

It can also show how effectively various elements of the marketing mix contribute to the overall effort. Suppose television ads have a 25 percent greater impact than radio or cinema, which costs 60 percent less. In that case, managers can carry on a debate grounded in hard numbers rather than impressions or prejudices as to which media channels merit increased investment.

Marketing mix analysis can highlight those activities with the highest ROI while it flags the ones that are likely to show negative or mediocre returns. Especially in difficult economic times, it is essential to know which activities are working well. All too often, a downturn in the economy is taken as a signal to make drastic cuts in the marketing budget without doing a disciplined review of risks and opportunities. Numerous studies have shown that cutting marketing investment during a recession can cause more harm than good as any analysis-driven decisions are not reactionary.

Establish Accountability

marketing activities are designed to increase awareness of a brand and others and introduce a new product; still, others encourage repeat buying and build brand loyalty. Despite this division of labor, many companies evaluate their marketing campaigns by looking solely at sales, as if the marketing effort were a single-faceted activity.

Here is one place where marketing executives can take a lesson from human resource personnel. Just as key performance indicators (KPIs) are established, measured, and validated for people working for a company, so the elements of a marketing campaign must be put to the test. And as the KPIs are established and people are rewarded for reaching or surpassing performance goals, the marketing campaign's various activities can be incentivized. For instance, managers can link investment in television advertising to shifts in brand awareness. If the brand currently has 60 percent awareness, they might specify that TV advertising must increase that awareness to 70 percent. Once that goal is reached, they could continue to set incremental increases, accompanied by appropriate awards.

Alternatively, suppose that marketers plan to attach an instant purchase coupon to the larger-sized packets of their products to encourage greater consumption. If the average family's family's son of a product is 1.5 kg per month, a special consumer-promotion activity could be held responsible for increasing this amount to 2 kg a month. Similar links could be established, say, between direct-mail activities and household penetration.

The important matter is to establish reasonable, reachable – and appropriate – goals for each marketing activity, specify clearly what those goals are, and reward each element appropriately if it achieves the desired outcome. In combination with ROI analysis, tracking interim "brand he "lth." measur "s will create a more robust program.

Reallocate Marketing Resources to Capitalize on New Growth In some companies, and resource allocation is based on who shouts the loudest. Others conduct detailed planning exercises at the country or category level, but few look across countries and categories. This fractured view prevents optimization. How does France's country manager compare her opportunity to better or worse opportunities in Germany or Spain? How does the toothpaste category manager compare his opportunity to better or worse opportunities in shampoo or deodorant?

Many companies find this step the most difficult to implement because they rely on ineffective ways of allocating resources. It's too often a mait's of rewarding business units based on last year's year's' another case of the rearview mirror approach). Or managers allocate resources on the basis of a brand's brand' market size. Neither achieves his full potential as the investment – too much or too little – hinders proper growth. To make matters worse, an under-rewarded business unit may find that the resources it receives fall below a minimum threshold of required investment and that, accordingly, the investment is wasted.

Systems and processes must be put in place to quantify and compare investment opportunities in an "applet" apple" fashion." This equation's practical side is often hard to implement since reallocating resources may mean losing jobs, products, plants, or even an entire brand. Managers rewarded for growing their business measures fight for higher-than-appropriate resources. If, for example, a business unit currently accounts for only 3 percent of the company' company' but it can be shown that this unit should and could account for 6 percent shortly, the forward-looking manager will direct an appropriate amount (perhaps as much as 6 percent) of marketing resources to that opportunity now rather than waiting for growth that depends on that investment.

The problem is that this investment will probably come from a larger business with less future potential. However, the current larger business can defend today's easier than a growing (probably less profitable) business can. A data-driven process is required to ensure that growth is optimized.

A system and process based on investing today proportionally to future profit growth potential would represent a radical improvement for most companies.

CONCLUSION

Strategic development and marketing creativity can thrive in an environment based on a strong commitment to maximizing profits. The focus on customer's and relationship management has always been about a better way to increase long-term profitability. Used in combination with more advanced ROI measurement and planning techniques, these strategies can be guided toward more effective integration, streamlined decision making, and effective investment management. Companies with superior processes for managing profitability can gain competitive advantages and provide better returns to employees, customers, and investors.

There are many paths to profitability. The traditional paths are well marked and familiar but include unnecessary detours that are costly. Big gains in profitability require taking some less familiar paths and forging some new paths. The marketing organization is responsible for motivating customer's from the first impression through a lifetime of repeat purchases. It's unacceptable that billions of dollars are being wasted each year on ineffective marketing initiatives in today's competitive environment. Without question, smarter marketing can generate more profitable returns, so it's time to manage the budget as an investment and not an expense. It will take champions at every level of the organization to establish the passion, processes, and practices necessary to deliver more profits.